COURTROOM'S FINEST HOUR IN AMERICAN CINEMA

by

Thomas J. Harris

The Scarecrow Press, Inc.
Metuchen, N.J., & London
1987

The author gratefully acknowledges permission to reprint the following:

Excerpts from Donald Spoto's Stanley Kramer: Film Maker (New York: G.P. Putnam's Sons, 1978). Reprinted by permission of Donald Spoto. Copyright © 1978 by Donald Spoto.

Excerpts from Aric Press' "The Verdict: A Legal Opinion," Newsweek (February 28, 1983). Reprinted by permission of Newsweek, Inc.

Excerpts from Robert Traver's Introduction to Anatomy of a Murder, 25th anniversary edition (New York: St. Martin's Press, 1983). Copyright © 1983 by Robert Traver.

Library of Congress Cataloging-in-Publication Data

Harris, Thomas J., 1966–
    Courtroom's finest hour in American cinema.

    Includes index.
    1. Trials in motion pictures. 2. Moving-
pictures--United States. I. Title.
PN1995.9.T75H37 1987 791.43'09'09355   86–26073
ISBN 0-8108-1956-2

In memory of Otto Preminger,

whose brilliant film <u>Anatomy of a Murder</u>

was the inspiration for this book

(Photo courtesy of Sigma Productions, Inc.)

CONTENTS

FOREWORD

I have always felt that I was very fortunate to get a part in the picture "ANATOMY OF A MURDER." Otto Preminger is one of the best. There was an excellent cast, and the script was extra special.

I think probably the most unusual part of my experience up in Ishpeming, Michigan, was that we were shooting the picture in the exact places that the story itself took place. This, I'd never experienced before and it made it a very fine experience.

James Stewart

ACKNOWLEDGMENTS

Many individuals deserve credit for making this endeavor possible, and I would like to take this opportunity to extend my appreciation to them.

My thanks go to Stanley Kramer, Wendell Mayes, Richard Murphy, Richard Fleischer, John Voelker, and Reginald Rose for answering my questions about the films and for offering general encouragement. Special thanks to James Stewart for taking time from his incredibly busy schedule to read the Anatomy chapter for me and to offer his thoughts on the picture.

I am also grateful to Otto Preminger's office for supplying me with a photo of him during what must have been a very painful period, and to the staffs of the UCLA Film Stills Archive, The Museum of Modern Art Film Stills Archive, and Collectors' Book Store in Hollywood for helping me locate stills.

I thank Robert Kaplow for reading the manuscript and for suggesting changes where necessary.

My gratitude is extended to Maureen McAndrew, Melissa King, Don Chang, and Joe Strupp for offering encouragement throughout the long, lonely, and sometimes tedious process of preparing the manuscript. I would also like to thank David Wang not only for supplying me with the above, but also for helping with the preparation of the index.

And, of course, to my family, without whom....

T.J.H.

INTRODUCTION

"In what other forum besides a courtroom could battles for such awesomely high stakes as freedom and sometimes life itself be fought in such a muted atmosphere of hushed ritual and controlled decorum, one so awash with ancient rites and Latinized locutions, one so filled with such obeisant rhetorical antiquities as 'If it please Your Honor' and all the rest?"

So pondered Michigan Supreme Court Justice John D. Voelker, better known as Robert Traver, author of Anatomy of a Murder, the best-seller that was turned into one of the films featured in this book.

It seems that Americans' love affair with the sorts of rituals which Mr. Traver describes dates back to the late 1920s and early 1930s, when films like Madame X, Counsellor at Law, and The Life of Emile Zola proved big hits at box offices all across the country.

Despite the popularity of these early courtroom-related pictures with audiences, however, they ultimately proved to be little more than mildly diverting entertainments, with virtually no redeeming social significance. Thus, the question, What makes a strong courtroom picture? comes to mind. Foremost in one's list of criteria would undoubtedly be, in addition to social commentary, meaty character study and an honest, uncompromising viewpoint on one particular aspect of the judicial system.

The courtroom films made in America between the mid-1950s and mid-1960s seem to provide the greatest opportunity for examining social problems of the past and present and for making statements about the validity of the judicial process. Some of these pictures represent definitive treatments of real-life cases (I Want to Live!, Barbara Graham; Compulsion, Leopold & Loeb; Inherit the Wind, Scopes Monkey Trial; Judgment at Nuremberg, Nazi War Crimes Trials), while others are loosely based on actual events (12 Angry Men, Anatomy of a Murder).

The decade stretching from approximately 1965 to 1975 saw the courtroom drama literally vanish from sight, as concern with society's deviants (Easy Rider, 1969; Five Easy Pieces, 1970), with crime (Dirty Harry, 1971; the two Godfather sagas, 1972 and 1974; and Death Wish, 1974), and with countless disaster epics (Poseidon Adventure, 1972; Towering Inferno, 1974; Airport films, 1969-79) represented the course of American films. However, 1982 saw new hope arise for the socially conscious courtroomer, as The Verdict became an instant hit with the public. My chapter on The Verdict takes the place of the decidedly inferior And Justice for All (1979) and The Star Chamber (1983) in summing up the attitude of societal pessimism in America of the eighties.

Of course, not all courtroom pictures are concerned with making statements, but are simply impeccable entertainments, impossible to resist. For this reason I have included a chapter on Billy Wilder's film version of Christie's Witness for the Prosecution, probably the most popular courtroom drama of all time, and one which replaces the countless mediocre productions of the thirties and forties.

I was amazed to discover that the subject of courtroom cinema has not even been touched in the thirty-odd years since film scholarship began to be taken seriously in this country and abroad. This is especially astonishing to me in light of the great commercial success which most of these films have enjoyed over the years and also since they represent high points in the careers of their directors (Sidney Lumet, Billy Wilder, Robert Wise, Otto Preminger, Stanley Kramer) and stars (Henry Fonda, who repeatedly confessed that 12 Angry Men was his favorite among his films; Susan Hayward, in her Oscar-winning role as Barbara Graham in I Want to

Live!; Charles Laughton in Witness for the Prosecution; Orson Welles as Darrow in Compulsion; Spencer Tracy as Darrow
and Fredric March as William Jennings Bryan in Inherit the
Wind; and James Stewart and George C. Scott, both Academy
Award nominees for Anatomy of a Murder).

Despite the fact that all of these pictures provide hard-
hitting entertainment and (with the exception of Witness for
the Prosecution) perceptive social commentary, the reader
must keep two things in mind. First, these are, after all,
feature films and not documentaries, so the facts, however
true to life they may seem, are always presented in a sub-
jective manner which reflects the biases of the filmmaker.
And finally, the films by and large contain resolutions which
are ultimately ambiguous in nature, requiring the reader to
become, in effect, the jury; indeed, that's why they represent the finest hour of the courtroom cinema in America.

Chapter 1

12 ANGRY MEN

Credits

An Orion/Nova Production, released through United Artists,
1957. Coproducers: Henry Fonda and Reginald Rose. Di-
rector: Sidney Lumet. Story and Screenplay: Reginald Rose.
Director of Photography: Boris Kaufman, A.S.C. Editor:
Carl Lerner. Art Director: Robert Markell. Music: Kenyon
Hopkins. Assistant Producer: George Justin. Assistant Di-
rector: Donald Kranze. Operative Cameraman: Saul Midwall.
Sound: James A. Gleason. Script Supervisor: Faith Elliott.
Makeup: Herman Buchman. Black-and-white. Running time:
96 minutes.

Cast: Henry Fonda (Juror 8), Lee J. Cobb (Juror 3), Ed
Begley (Juror 10), E.G. Marshall (Juror 4), Jack Warden
(Juror 7), Martin Balsam (Juror 1), John Fiedler (Juror 2),
Jack Klugman (Juror 5), Joseph Sweeney (Juror 9), Edward
Binns (Juror 6), George Voskovec (Juror 11), Robert Webber
(Juror 12), Rudy Bond (Judge), James A. Kelly (Guard),
Bill Nelson (Court Clerk), John Savoca (Defendant).

It is convenient that the first chapter of this book on
courtroom cinema should center on the most pivotal aspect of
a trial--the jury: with a thorough understanding of its intricacies, the reader will be able to appreciate better the statements made by the writers and directors of the films to come
regarding the reliability of the judicial system in general.

1

Strangely enough, as of 1957 the subject of the jury had only received one serious treatment in all of world cinema--by French writer-director Andre Cayette in his 1950 film Justice est Faite (Let Justice Be Done), which explored the extent to which the personal lives of the jury members in a mercy killing affected their verdict. Its main point was that the attainment of absolute impartiality is impossible in a jury situation, to which people unavoidably carry with them deep-seated prejudices and convictions.

Some three years after the release of the Cayette film in France, a young American TV writer named Reginald Rose found himself confronting precisely the same dilemmas that had plagued Cayette's characters when he was asked to serve on a New York jury. Rose was so affected by his experience that he fashioned a teleplay from it. When "12 Angry Men," as it was called, aired in early 1954, it proved an immediate critical and commercial hit--its potency of theme appearing all the more credible due to its basis on actual events.

Two years later, in 1956, Rose was asked by Henry Fonda, who had seen the TV production of "12 Angry Men" and who was looking for a commercial property over which he could serve as producer as well as a starring vehicle for himself, to expand his teleplay to feature length. This practice had become fairly common during the 1950s, what with the number of original story ideas for motion pictures steadily declining. Producers had begun to turn to their greatest rival, television, for new material. Paddy Chayefsky's TV plays "Marty" and "The Bachelor Party" were both transferred to the screen in 1955 and 1957, respectively, by their original director, Delbert Mann. Since television was primarily a writer's (although to a great extent an actor's) medium, it was wisely decided that the screen adaptations of these teleplays would rely heavily on dialogue, in addition to the other fundamentals of television: "a narrative style based on medium close-ups ... a highly mobile camera enclosed within a limited space and the intimate quality of ... situations."[1]

These films were also made at low costs, because they utilized television crews instead of motion picture crews (Alfred Hitchcock was to discover just how cheaply a feature film could be made in 1960 when, using the crew from his TV show, he produced and directed Psycho, his top-grossing film of all time, for a mere $800,000).

Sidney Lumet directs his first feature, 12 Angry Men.

The man chosen to direct the screen version of "12 Angry Men" was Sidney Lumet, who was still a novice to movies (hard to believe from today's standpoint) but who was well-experienced in TV, having directed episodes for such popular series as "You Are There," "Playhouse 90," "Kraft Television Theatre," and "Studio One." In addition, most of the acting ensemble was drawn from among the ranks of TV performers: E.G. Marshall, Jack Warden, Edward Binns, John Fiedler, Martin Balsam, among others.

12 Angry Men opens on a steamy summer afternoon in a courtroom inside Manhattan's Court of General Sessions. A judge is wearily grumping his charge to an equally dog-tired and heat-soaked jury: first-degree manslaughter with a death penalty mandatory upon a guilty verdict. However, he reminds them, to send the defendant (a slum boy) to the chair their verdict of guilty must be unanimous; if there exists in

any juror's mind a reasonable doubt as to the guilt or innocence of the accused, a vote of not guilty must be entered.
As the jury remove themselves from the box, the viewer is
shown a lingering close-up of the frightened boy. Kenyon
Hopkins' grim, sympathetic theme (which will recur each
time a life-or-death situation is faced) continues until the
credits fade as the jury--and the audience--settle themselves in that sweltering broom closet for the next hour
and a half. Already Rose has established the contrast between the slum kid of a minority race and the white, middle-
class males who have been selected to determine his fate.
We will soon discover that the defendant in the case is not
only the boy on trial but also the jury and, in a broader
sense, the judicial system itself.

Once inside the jury room, the men are introduced to
the viewer as they talk among themselves about how "open-
and-shut" the case against the boy seems. Assuming the
airs of the intelligent, respectable citizens they presume
themselves to be, they never for a moment doubt the validity of their convictions, but instead speak of how "exciting"
the trial was or of the stifling atmosphere of the room (they
are unable to get the fan to work) or of how the proceedings
have rudely interrupted their daily routines (one is anxious
to get to the ball park). They act as though they've seen
it all before; in fact, one of them later says to Henry Fonda,
who casts the only vote for not-guilty, "You couldn't change
my mind if you talked for a hundred years." However, by
the end of the film all eleven of them will have been per-
suaded by Fonda to open their minds to the possibility of
the existence of a reasonable doubt in the case.

Juror 1 (Martin Balsam) is chosen to be the foreman.
He is a high-school gym teacher, about 30, somewhat dumb
and weak-willed, and extremely sensitive--when someone objects to one of his decisions, he says, "All right, then do it
yourself. See how you like being in charge." His opinions
will be overlooked while the other eleven take over. In
short, he is a foreman by name only.

Juror 2 (John Fiedler) is a wimpy bank teller of about
35. He (like some of the others) is used to having decisions
made for him and enjoys going along with the majority so
he'll look good and won't have to stand up for himself.
Whatever views he has are usually silenced by the more

aggressive types in the group. However, he does make an
effort to maintain the level of interpersonal contact among
the men when arguments ensue by offering cough drops.

Juror 3 (Lee J. Cobb) is a husky, loud-mouthed,
domineering bully who runs a messenger service. He states
in the beginning that he has no personal feelings about the
case, but we eventually learn that his own teenaged son has
deserted him and for that reason he is taking out his anger
on the defendant. His blind desire to side with anyone who
is ready to convict the boy allows Fonda and the others on
his side to come up with new evidence to support the theory
that there exists a reasonable doubt concerning the boy's
guilt.

Juror 4 (E.G. Marshall), the stockbroker, is a cold-
blooded (so much so that he says he never sweats) rationalist who treats the whole case as if it were a detective puzzle
and not a question of whether a human being is going to live
or die. "Studies confirm that slum kids are potential criminals," he declares. He is conceited and stuffy and does not
hesitate to tell the others what he thinks of them whenever
the opportunity arises. He is, however, obviously a good
producer of information and has excellent recall, and is help-
ful in that respect at least.

Juror 5 (Jack Klugman) is an insecure victim of a slum
upbringing. He is not a mean man, but would vote in favor
of the boy's guilt simply because discussing the details of a
case with many parallels to his own childhood is too much
for his conscience to bear. However, once he has come to
grips with his past, he is eager to assist Fonda and the
others in reevaluating the case against the boy.

Juror 6 (Edward Binns) is a working-class "Joe" more
inclined toward using his hands than his brains. "I'm not
used to supposing," he tells Fonda. "My boss does that for
me." He provides a facilitation function in the group--that
is, he tries to make things go smoothly--as when he badgers
the bully for silencing Juror 9, the old man: "You say stuff
like that to him again, and I'll lay you out."

Juror 7's (Jack Warden) only desire is to get out of
his seat in the jury room and into one at the ball park. In
fact, he is so completely obsessed with baseball that he makes

unconscious references to it in virtually everything he says;
he calls Juror 5 "Baltimore" because of his attachment to the
Orioles; he tells the foreman to "just stand there and pitch"
when he says something irritating; he recites the ratio of
guilty to not-guilty votes as if it were a player's hit-and-
miss record. He is perhaps the most alarming figure in the
whole group because he has absolutely no concern for the
defendant's welfare. He preoccupies himself with cracking
jokes and performing stupid acts like throwing paper balls
at the fan. When Fonda finally secures a majority of not-
guilty votes, he switches his vote to not-guilty simply to
facilitate the establishment of a unanimous verdict; he has
no convictions either way. That he appears amusing on the
surface seems all the more appalling when one reflects upon
the seriousness of the situation which he's making light of.

Juror 9 (Joseph Sweeney), the old man, needs moral
support, for he has an inferiority complex. Fortunately,
Fonda, the working man, and some of the others manage to
see to it that he gets the floor once in a while despite the
dominance of the loudmouths in the group. In spite of his
years, however, he is extremely perceptive, and some of his
observations--unseen by any of the others--result in alter-
ing the opinions of a few of the more stubborn among the
men.

Juror 10 (Ed Begley) is a garage owner who is absolutely seething with racial prejudice. "They're all the same
--can't trust any of 'em--know what I mean?" is his recur-
rent statement with regard to the boy's ethnic background.
He is nasty and quick to accuse (when Fonda is the only
one to vote not-guilty at the beginning, he immediately
snickers, "Boyoboy, there's always one"). Although he
acts tough, it becomes increasingly clear that his rantings
and ravings last only as long as there are supporters to
urge him on.

Juror 11 (George Voskovec), a German-American, is
an immigrant watchmaker who initially votes guilty simply
because his reverence for the principles of American justice
has blinded him into believing that the system is infallible:
the boy seems guilty, therefore he must be. He is somewhat
arrogant but is rightfully angered at the baseball fan's in-
difference and the bully's rudeness. By standing up for
his beliefs he gives direction to the group.

Juror 12 (Robert Webber) is an ad man accustomed to making decisions for appearance's sake. He has no deep-seated convictions regarding the guilt or innocence of the boy and as a result has difficulty making up his mind when his opinion is needed to break a tie vote.

From an examination of these men it becomes clear that Rose has chosen a pretty fair cross-section of society to fill his jury. After they are certain that they've given the case a thorough evaluation (they've talked for all of five minutes), one calls to the man (Juror 8, Henry Fonda) who has been standing alone by the window. Fonda has been thinking the case over in his mind, not worrying about his own problems. The contrast between him and his fellow jurors is firmly established when a vote is taken and he is the only one who raises his hand for not-guilty. After the others have somewhat tempered their initial hostility, they agree to explain to him why they think he should change his mind. It must be pointed out that he has not voted not-guilty because he is sure the boy is innocent, but because there exists in his

Fonda trying to persuade the other jurors.

mind a reasonable doubt as to guilt. The law states that
this is all that is necessary for acquittal.

After a once-around-the-table, it becomes obvious that
no one has given the case much thought. "I just think he's
guilty ... the evidence all seemed to point in that direction,"
are the empty generalizations spouted by these eleven men
who are prepared to send a boy to the chair without even a
second thought.

Since it is evident that they would rather ignore Fonda
and wait for him to "come to his senses" than try to help
him see their point of view, Fonda realizes that it is up to
him to convince them that there is room for reasonable doubt.
He has his work cut out for him, though, for he must contend with the hostility of the others in the group--the garage mechanic in particular--who are growing more and more
impatient.

It is already clear to the viewer that Fonda is the only
man present who is not indifferent and who has not allowed
personal prejudice to obscure his perception of the case.
He is also apparently the only one with a lucid understanding of the judicial process--and the one with the most common sense. He has to remind the bank teller that the burden of proof is on the prosecution, not the defense. He
cleverly makes the ad man contradict his belief that witnesses
who say things under oath cannot be wrong by getting him
to admit, "This isn't an exact science."

Nevertheless, for all his effort, Fonda elicits nothing
but jeers from those to whom he points out shortcomings in
reasoning. Discouraged, but secretly hoping that he has
penetrated the stubborn veneer of at least one of the other
jurors, he agrees to another vote--but this time on secret
ballot, with himself abstaining. He says that if the outcome
is a unanimous guilty vote, he will not stand in their way;
however, if there is one vote for not-guilty among them,
then they must stay and talk it out. He is taking a great
risk by placing his confidence in this largely ignorant and
biased bunch.

Fortunately, there is one vote for not-guilty (we later
discover that it came from the old man). Reluctantly, the
other members of the jury set out to reexamine the case.

Fonda's task from this point on will be to convince the other ten that there is a question of doubt regarding the case of the defendant. Because he is a keen judge of character, he avoids pleading his cause directly to the most seemingly intractable types--the baseball fan, the garage owner, and the messenger-service operator--and instead concentrates on the more reasonable types--the working man, the slum kid, the bank teller, etc. He knows that once they begin to accept him as a leader, he will be able to break down the stronghold of personal prejudice that the others possess. It should be mentioned at this point that there are many temporary leaders in the group; practically everyone gets the floor once in a while. Leadership is a function, not a position. However, Fonda becomes the strongest and most influential leader because he manages to gain the support of the others in the group; lasting leadership demands followers. Fonda's unfaltering independence of judgment will gradually strengthen the independence of judgment of the others. One by one, the other jurors will begin to realize how close they came to sending a boy to die due to their indifferent attitudes.

Fonda begins to introduce pieces of evidence that throw doubt upon the so-called "open-and-shut" appearance of the case against the boy. He confounds the other jurors when he produces a knife identical to the one with which the boy allegedly stabbed his father. His point is that someone else could have bought the knife, as he did, at a store in the boy's neighborhood and used it to kill the boy's father. "It's possible, but not very probable," declares the stockbroker in his usual perfunctory tone. Nevertheless, it is still to Fonda's credit that he was concerned enough to give up some of his free time to search the boy's area, whereas the others never gave the knife a second thought because it was an unusual-looking instrument and seemed to be one of a kind.

Fonda also brings up the crucial question of the accuracy of the testimony of the lame old man who said that he got up from his seat in his bedroom after hearing what he thought were screams, went to the front door immediately, opened it, and saw the boy running past. Using a diagram of the man's apartment and imitating his movements while clocking them, Fonda shows that it would have been impossible for the handicapped witness to walk forty feet from his bedroom to the door in the twelve seconds he said

Fonda reveals the knife.

it took him to do so. It would have taken him at least three
times that long. Therefore, it is highly probable that the
man merely heard someone running past and assumed it was
the boy. Earlier, Fonda had reasoned that the old man's
statement that he heard the boy say he was going to kill his
father would have meant that the shouts were picked up over
the deafening roar of an L-train. When Juror 3 asked what
difference it made how many seconds it took before the old
man heard the screams, that no one could be that positive,
Fonda had replied, "I think that testimony that could send
a boy to the chair should be as accurate as seconds." This
points up another major concern of the film--the reliability
of the testimony of people who are, after all, only human

and therefore prone to making mistakes. Just because someone says something under oath does not necessarily signify
that it is unquestionable. Sometimes people say things for
appearance's sake--as Juror 9 points out when he says that
the old man on the stand may have been making an effort to
look distinguished for possibly the first time in his life and
that as a result he may have deliberately twisted the facts.
Even the persons with superior recall--and there are not
many in the group--are not totally reliable--as we will discover later with regard to the stockbroker. However, the
other jurors' excessive faith in the accuracy of the judicial
process would have them believe that human error somehow
becomes nonexistent once a person enters a court of law.
The question of what motivates a witness' testimony will be
explored again in Witness for the Prosecution and most extensively (and realistically) in Anatomy of a Murder.

Apparently Fonda's efforts have not gone unrewarded,
for the next vote finds the count 8 guilty to 4 not-guilty,
as opposed to the original 11 to 1; the watchmaker has now
changed his mind. It is at this point that Juror 3, who has
been castigating those who have sided with Fonda ("You
bunch of bleedin' hearts ... what is this--Love Your Under-
privileged Brother Week or something?") allows all his latent
hostility with regard to his runaway son to surface:

> Juror 3: You're letting him slip through our
> fingers!
>
> Fonda: Slip through our fingers?! Who are you,
> his executioner?
>
> Juror 3 (clenching his fist): I'm one of 'em.
>
> Fonda: Perhaps you'd like to pull the switch.
>
> Juror 3: For this kid, you bet I would.
>
> Fonda (contemptuously): I feel sorry for you.
> What it must feel like to want to pull the switch.
> Ever since you came in here you've been acting
> like a self-appointed public avenger.... You're
> a sadist. [2]

During this exchange all the other jurors have gathered around Fonda and have been staring, astonished, at
Juror 3; he has been singled out, just as Fonda was the

Fonda confronts Cobb: "You're a sadist." (Photo courtesy of Museum of Modern Art/Film Stills Archive)

first time we saw him. These two are clearly the most dia-metrically opposed individuals in the room. Juror 3 lunges at Fonda, declaring, "I'll kill him." Fonda, defiantly: "You don't really mean you'll kill me, do you?" And Juror 3 real-izes that Fonda is right. From this point on, Juror 3 ap-pears more introspective--he speaks out less often--but still retains his angry facade. His outburst has also caused the other jurors who voted guilty to ask themselves whether they have similar prejudices which are preventing them from changing their perspectives. They are again given pause to reflect after the watchmaker's awe-inspired speech about the merits of the American jury process: "We have nothing to gain or lose by our verdict. We don't know the boy" (even though Juror 10 would contend, "They're all the same"). The next vote is a tie: 6-6.

At about this time the frustrated and exhausted men

are given relief by a downpour. The rain acts to reduce
the tension: it cools the intense emotional atmosphere of
the room as well as the men themselves. By the next vote,
Fonda has secured a majority: 9 not-guilty to 3 guilty.
The three dissenters are the bully, the stockbroker, and
the bigot. Fonda demands that they state their reasons for
holding onto their conviction. The stockbroker's smug attitude is finally broken down by Fonda and the old man. The
rationalist had refused to believe that the boy couldn't remember the names of the films he allegedly saw the night his
father was murdered. However, when Fonda confronts the
stockbroker with a similar question, the latter finds his usually infallible memory failing him; he cannot name all the
stars in the double-feature he saw three nights ago. Fonda:
"And you're not under emotional stress [as the boy was],
are you?" The old man notices the stockbroker rubbing the
marks on the sides of his nose and remembers that the woman
who testified against the boy had been doing the same thing:
in both cases the marks were caused by glasses (and nothing
else, as the stockbroker himself admits), but the woman on
the stand, in an effort to look younger, was not wearing
hers. It is also deduced by the stockbroker that she would
not have been wearing them to bed on the night she heard
screams in the boy's apartment. Therefore, in the split
second she said it took her to jump out of bed and look out
the window through the cars of a passing L-train (at which
point she said she saw the boy knife his father) it is highly
unlikely that she took time to put on her glasses (her ne-
glecting to wear them to court confirms that she is not in
the habit of using them). Fonda concludes that she couldn't
have been certain about what she saw under those circumstances. Finally, the stockbroker admits that there is room
for reasonable doubt and changes his vote to not-guilty.

Next, the bigot, who is absolutely fed up with the
"soft hearts" of the other jurors, launches his longest tirade
against minorities. Everyone demonstrates how intolerant
they have grown of his attitudes when they get up from the
table and turn their backs to him, leaving him babbling in
vain in the middle of the room. Evidently without others to
fuel the fire of his racism, it soon dies out. When the stockbroker tells him, "Sit down and don't open your mouth again,"
he obsequiously complies. For the remaining period, he sits
quietly by himself in a corner of the room, most likely con-
templating for the first time the ludicrousness of his prejudiced views.

Henry Fonda in action. (Photo courtesy of Museum of Modern Art/Film Stills Archive)

A tense moment between Fonda and Cobb. (Photo courtesy
of Museum of Modern Art/Film Stills Archive)

Finally the vote is reversed: 11 not-guilty to 1 guilty.
Now the Angry Man stands alone. He tries desperately to
get others to support him, but it is clear that his personal
problems are the only things keeping him from going along
with them. "You're trying to turn this into a contest," says
the stockbroker. Reginald Rose drops his final comment on
the unreliability of witness testimony when Juror 3, having
resorted to bringing up the presumably settled issue of the
vain woman who testified against the boy, shouts, "You can
talk all you want, but you can't prove she wasn't wearing
glasses. This woman testified in court." After all of Fonda's
efforts over the past hour and a half to illustrate the fact
that human weakness is present everywhere--even, perhaps
especially in court--and that things are not always what they
seem, the words "testified in court" have virtually lost all
their meaning. Realizing that he is getting nowhere, Juror 3
pulls out his wallet to show the others some "facts" that he

has presumably scribbled down--and out flies a picture of
him and his son together. He stares at it for a moment,
then uses all his pent up rage to tear it to shreds. Having
finally come to grips with his conscience, he sobs, "Not
guilty."

        The final moments show Fonda exiting the courthouse.
The old man stops him and asks him what his name is.
"Davis," he replies. "Well, so long," says the old man.
Here is another of Rose's subtle points: these men have
been sitting in a courtroom for ninety minutes without know-
ing much personal data about the others in the group outside
of their emotional temperaments and intellectual capacities
(they've all accepted each other as "normal"--all of them being white males), but they have judged the boy as though
they understood him completely, when in fact they know less
about him than they do about each other. The racist assumed he was untrustworthy because he was "one of them,"
and the bully envisioned him as having the same characteris-
tics as his rebellious son. Unfortunately, oftentimes people
are more inclined to let their emotions govern their decisions
than to use unbiased logical reasoning.

        We realize that the final exchange between Fonda and
the old man is a meaningless formality: they will probably
never see each other again. Looking back, we see that in
the beginning this group of diverse individuals was prepared
(with the exception of Fonda) to send a boy to the chair
and then go home and forget all about it. It is frightening
to consider just how close they came to doing so. It must
be stated, however, that the jury's final verdict of not-guilty
does not prove conclusively that the boy did not murder his
father; rather, the script shows that the case against the
boy is not as strong as the case for him--the presence of
reasonable doubt is Rose's concern. What if there had been
no Juror 8? Rose may be praised for his convincing account
of how a liberal man who is devoted to his cause is able to
sway the ignorant and prejudiced minds of his peers. However, at the same time it may be said that the script relies
too heavily upon the chance presence of such a man; if he
had not been there to point out evidence that no one else
had been able to produce, the boy would presumably have
been sent to the chair. It is also questionable whether such
a man, even if he happened to be present, would have the
stamina to enable him to ignore the incessant badgering of

his colleagues--as one character in the film remarks, "It isn't easy to stand up to the ridicule of others." Indeed, because the story "is based on the dramatically convenient but otherwise simplistic assumption that people's prejudices can be traced to specific occurrences in their past and can thereby be accounted for and removed ... the Fonda character had to come on as a combination Sherlock Holmes and Perry Mason, as well as double as confessor, catalyst, and instant psychiatrist to a number of the jurors."[3] Also, due to the great reliance upon Fonda's presence, details are exposed and clarified much too smoothly. It is only Fonda who employs logical reasoning most of the time, and even when someone else brings up a point it usually comes as the result of Fonda's questioning. It may also be stated that, as Adam Garbicz and Jacek Klinowski remark in their article on the film in Cinema: The Magic Vehicle, "the actors are hardly a team, but rather a group of diverse individuals against whom Henry Fonda shines with all the more brightness."[4] The subordination of details to suit a single star role would also mar the effectiveness of another courtroom drama of the 50s, Robert Wise's I Want to Live! (1958), as we shall see in Chapter 3.

In addition to the issue of the omniscience of the Fonda character, the script eschews realism for dramatic convenience in other respects also. Juror 3's sudden emotional breakdown, for example, remains largely unconvincing because it is triggered by the chance appearance of a photo of him and his son when he throws the wallet down on the table. Since all the others have sided with Fonda, Rose is left with no alternative but to find a quick and easy method for getting Juror 3 to do the same.

Nevertheless, Rose does manage to point out ironic truths abouth the judicial system on a reasonably frequent basis. There is, for example, the bigot's complaint that the old man is "twisting the facts" when he says that the elderly gentleman on the stand gave testimony mainly to look distinguished. Since the jurors are not the people on the stand, they cannot know what the witnesses are thinking; hence, the truth is often never revealed. The best the jury can do is try to read between the lines and make intelligent guesses; however, we have seen that initially no one except Fonda even considered the possibility of testimony being inaccurate.

There is also the fact that the presence of certain individuals in the jury room can alter the course of events.
No one except Juror 5, who was once a slum kid, knows how
a switchblade is handled. He demonstrates how awkward it
would have been for the boy, who was much shorter than
his father, to stab upward into the chest. The old man,
preoccupied with studying people his own age, deduces from
his observations of the vain woman in the witness box that
she wasn't wearing her glasses.

Rose leaves it up to the viewer whether the experience
of being a jury member has changed the characters of the
men who have been shown their true selves as a result. It
appears as though the bigot and the bully have confronted
deep-seated personal conflicts for the first time in their lives.
One wonders, however, whether the lessons they learned in
court will have a long-term effect on their perceptions of the
world.

Although Rose's script has its shortcomings, there is
no denying that it is brilliantly tight, that it makes for ex-
hilarating drama, and that it is food for thought. However,
it is director Lumet who deserves credit for bringing Rose's
words to life. For his success in overcoming the otherwise
inevitable static quality of such an enclosed situation enough
cannot be said. His camera probes those four walls relent-
lessly; of the 375 shots of the film, almost all were taken
from a different angle.[5] Throughout, he heightens dramatic
tension and creates suspense by using extreme (and often
grotesque) close-ups and by illuminating subtle nuances of
character. For instance, after Juror 3 finishes telling the
others about his runaway son the first time, the camera
continues to keep him in the right foreground, alone and in
silent meditation, as the proceedings continue. The stockbroker early on tells Juror 5 that he never sweats; yet, after listening to the old man's revealing speech about the
woman's glasses, we see him quickly take out a handkerchief
and wipe his brow.

Lumet and his cinematographer, Boris Kaufman, constantly emphasize the claustrophobic atmosphere of the drab,
cramped, stuffy jury room. The sound of someone coughing or

[Opposite:]   The bigot stands alone.

sneezing often blocks out another's dialogue. The uncomfortable physical environment matches the emotional tensions generated by the discussion. Kaufman, by the way, was by this time well-accustomed to shooting in real locations (12 Angry Men was shot in an actual jury room): he had photographed Elia Kazan's On the Waterfront (1954) on the docks of Hoboken and Baby Doll (1956) in the decaying Southern atmosphere of Benoit, Mississippi. Kaufman would later assist Lumet on That Kind of Woman (1959), The Fugitive Kind (1960), Long Day's Journey into Night (1962), The Pawnbroker (1965), The Group (1966) and Bye Bye Braverman (1968).

Finally, there are the performances. The whole ensemble is expert and thoroughly credible (indeed, this could be said for most of the films of Lumet's early career, characterized as it was by group situations), but the more prominent players must be singled out. Lee J. Cobb brought his muscular Johnny Friendly presence from On the Waterfront to his portrayal of the vengeful bully and again seemed singularly suited for his role. Ed Begley made a thoroughly repellent racist. Henry Fonda once again proved himself to be the epitome of the decent, honest, soft-spoken liberal. Lumet would return Fonda's favor by using him in two subsequent features, Stage Struck (1958) and Fail-Safe (1964).

In terms of cinematic execution, 12 Angry Men was clearly a film of its time. It is probable that if it were made today under the same conditions (with a TV crew and at TV speed), audiences who have since come to accept motion pictures and television as two unique forms of entertainment--with much higher standards for films--would dismiss it as a laughable "gimmick" film despite the gravity of its messages.

Nevertheless, after nearly thirty years 12 Angry Men remains one of the most absorbing exposes of the workings of the judicial process. This is due mainly to Rose's penetrating indictment of the reliability of the jury system. Lumet's contribution was pretty much technical (although his direction of the actors was superlative); indeed, what with the challenge of having to complete the shooting in a mere twenty days, he could hardly have been expected to develop any sort of personal philosophy. Although the film ends on a happy note, the viewer (as mentioned before) is

inescapably reminded of the more serious implications of the
previous ninety minutes: the extent to which personal biases
can taint a juror's perceptions of the real issues and as a result endanger the lives of the (presumably innocent) parties
on trial. Even though Rose, like Cayette in Justice est Faite,
does not offer alternatives to the present system of trial by
jury, his screenplay is, on the whole, a more fervent and
angered denunciation of the American public's idealistic approach to the reliability of the system. His message, that
"the law is no better than the people who enforce it, and
that the people who enforce it are all too human,"[6] is just
as pertinent today as it was in 1957.

NOTES

1. Adam Garbicz and Jacek Klinowski, Cinema, the Magic
    Vehicle: A Guide to its Achievement, vol. 2 (New York:
    Schocken Books, 1983), p. 251.

2. Reginald Rose, "Unpublished Screenplay for 12 Angry
    Men," (Orion-Nova Productions Inc., 1957). All refer-
    ences to dialogue come from here.

3. Jean-Pierre Coursodon and Pierre Sauvage, "Sidney
    Lumet," in American Directors, vol. 2 (New York:
    McGraw-Hill, 1983), p. 209.

4. Garbicz and Klinowski, p. 299.

5. Garbicz and Klinowski, p. 297.

6. Time, April 29, 1957, p. 96.

Chapter 2

WITNESS FOR THE PROSECUTION

Credits

An Arthur Hornblow Production for Theme Pictures, released through United Artists, 1958. An Edward Small Presentation. Producer: Arthur Hornblow, Jr. Director: Billy Wilder. Screenplay: Billy Wilder and Harry Kurnitz, based on Larry Marcus' adaptation of the story and play of the same name by Agatha Christie. Director of Photography: Russell Harlan. Editor: Daniel Mandell. Music: Matty Melneck, arranged by Leonid Raab and conducted by Ernest Gold. Song: "I May Never Go Home Any More"--music by Ralph Arthur Roberts and lyrics by Jack Brooks. Art Director: Alexander Trauner. Assistant Director: Emmett Emerson. Dietrich's Costumes: Edith Head. Costumes: Joseph Kin. Makeup: Ray Sebastian, Harry Rase, Gustaf Norin. Hairdressers: Helene Parris, Nellie Manley. Set Designer: Howard Bristol. Prop Master: Stanley Deflin. Sound: Fred Lau. Production Assistant: Doane Harrison. Production Manager: Ben Hersh. Script Supervisor: John Francis. Black-and-white. Running Time: 116 minutes.

Cast: Tyrone Power (Leonard Vole), Marlene Dietrich (Christine Vole), Charles Laughton (Sir Wilfrid Robarts), Elsa Lanchester (Miss Plimsoll), John Williams (Brogan-Moore), Henry Daniell (Mayhew), Ian Wolfe (Carter), Una O'Connor (Janet McKenzie), Torin Thatcher (Mr. Myers), Francis Compton (Judge), Norma Varden (Mrs. French),

Philip Tonge (Inspector Hearne), Ruta Lee (Diana), Molly
Roden (Miss McHugh), Ottola Nesmith (Miss Johnson), Mar-
jorie Eaton (Miss O'Brien), J. Pat O'Malley (Shorts Salesman).

Not all courtroom dramas, of course, are concerned
with making serious statements about the judicial system.
Some are just simply good entertainments, preoccupied with
illustrating how the conflict between lawyers and witnesses
can increase the suspense of the story.

Before the courtroom film began to be taken seriously--
that is, back in the late twenties and early thirties--this ob-
session with form over content prevailed. As could be expected, most of the courtroom-related films made during this
period were derived from popular stage plays--Bayard Veil-
ler's Trial of Mary Dugan (1929), Lionel Barrymore's Madame X (1929), and William Wyler's Counsellor at Law (1933),
to name a few. Of course, the narrative execution of most
of these early efforts now seems hopelessly antiquated. The
basically detached and indifferent Wyler who directed Counsellor at Law, for example, seems a different filmmaker entirely from the mature, meticulous personal artist who real-
ized The Best Years of Our Lives thirteen years later.

The point is that as the techniques of storytelling in
film grew more and more sophisticated, so too did the productions that resulted from this change. Stage plays were
still sought out as source material for motion pictures throughout the 1940s and 1950s, but the screen adaptations of these
dramas showed a decided improvement over their predecessors, mainly in light of their polished and professional execution.

Arthur Hornblow, Jr., producer of such popular hits
as John Huston's Asphalt Jungle (1950) and Fred Zinnemann's
Oklahoma! (1955), was on the verge of giving the courtroom
genre one of its finest achievements when he purchased the
screen rights to Agatha Christie's Witness for the Prosecution in the mid-1950s. Christie's whodunit about the trial
of a gentleman accused of murdering a rich widow had already been a favorite of readers and theater-goers both
British and American for more than a decade.

Upon hearing of Hornblow's acquisition of the property,

actress Marlene Dietrich, anxious to play the role of Christine, asked Billy Wilder to direct the film, certain that his
participation in the project would assure her obtaining the
part. Dietrich and Wilder had worked well together on Wilder's A Foreign Affair back in 1948. Throughout the 1950s
writer-director Wilder had been experimenting in a number
of different genres: cynical melodrama (Ace in the Hole,
1951), drama with comic asides (Stalag 17, 1953), comedy
with shades of social satire (The Seven Year Itch, 1955),
and, most recently, biography (The Spirit of St. Louis,
1957, with James Stewart playing Lindbergh). A courtroom
suspense story provided yet another unexplored area for
Wilder, and he gladly accepted the offer to direct the screen
version of Witness for the Prosecution. Incidentally, another
reason that Wilder wanted to make the film was that he and
Hornblow were good friends (Hornblow had produced Wilder's
first directorial effort, The Major and the Minor, back in
1942). Wilder also partly intended the picture to be a hom-
age to Alfred Hitchcock, whose flair for suspense he admired
very much. (Wilder's classic crime melodrama, Double Indem-

Leonard Vole (Tyrone Power) pleads with Sir Wilfrid Robarts
(Charles Laughton).

nity, 1944, contained several Hitchcockian touches, most
notably the car containing the murderers, Fred MacMurray
and Barbara Stanwyck, temporarily stalling at the scene of
the crime.)

Wilder's adaptation of Christie's play, which he wrote
with his friend Harry Kurnitz, being faithful to its source,
concerns itself mainly with the intricacies of plot rather than
with excessive character delineation. The first noticeable
change which Wilder imparted to the play is evident in the
very first scene. Sir Wilfrid Robarts (Charles Laughton),
one of London's most noted barristers, is returning to his
office after a lengthy absence following a heart attack. He
is accompanied by his ever-doting surrogate (or, rather,
"jailer," as he calls her), Miss Plimsoll (Elsa Lanchester),
who is determined to see to it that his activities from now
on do not involve harmful substances such as tobacco and
alcohol. Sir Wilfrid staunchly objects to this pampering and
is constantly making efforts to outwit her--at one point she
discovers that he has been hiding cigars in his cane. Wilder
invented this childlike conflict in order to provide a humor-
ous contrast to the seriousness of the situation facing the
accused man and his wife, Christine; Christie's original began with the man, Leonard Vole, being introduced to Sir
Wilfrid. Thus, the emphasis has been shifted from straight
drama to drama with comic asides.

At any rate, Sir Wilfrid is soon introduced to Vole
(Tyrone Power), the man suspected to having murdered a
rich widow, but, abiding by the wishes of Miss Plimsoll,
who objects to any strenuous activity on his part, he de-
clines to accept this case and hands it over to his attorney
friend Brogan-Moore (John Williams). However, Sir Wilfrid's
still-intense passion for the law soon gets the better of him
and, eluding his nurse, he rushes to his office to hear the
details of the case.

Leonard presents himself as a decent, industrious
young inventor who has been the victim of circumstance:
Wilder inserts a flashback which describes Leonard's chance
meeting with Mrs. French (Norma Varden), an elderly widow,
in a hatshop. It seems that the two of them soon became
good friends, to the point where, unbeknown to Leonard (or
so he says), she left him 80,000 pounds in her will--a fact,
as Sir Wilfrid points out, which will undoubtedly be used

Leonard in a flashback scene with Mrs. French (Norma Varden).

against him by the prosecution. Sir Wilfrid is easily won over by Leonard's sincere presentation. "Why, this man is simply not the killer type," he thinks to himself. However, Wilder cleverly foreshadows the truth about Leonard by having Robarts declare to him, after Leonard aids him in outwitting Miss Plimsoll, "You have all the instincts of a skilled criminal."

To Sir Wilfrid's astonishment, the one party whom he would certainly expect to be on Leonard's side, namely his wife, Christine (Marlene Dietrich), reveals that she is not really married to Leonard and furthermore that she has no sympathy for him. However, she says that since, as Sir Wilfrid points out, under English law a wife may not give incriminating testimony against her husband, she will support

Sir Wilfrid sneers at shorts salesman (J. Pat O'Malley) as
Miss Plimsoll (Elsa Lanchester) looks on.

him on the stand (by lying to the jury that she is Leonard's
wife). Sir Wilfrid, somewhat taken aback by her unabashed
admission that she will commit perjury while under oath if
necessary, warns her of the penalties for such an act. The
fact that her heart is not with Leonard worries him, especially when he discovers that Leonard is apparently oblivious to
her feelings toward him. Sir Wilfrid states, "His depending
on her is like a drowning man clutching at a razor blade."
When even Brogan-Moore expresses doubts as to his client's
innocence, Sir Wilfrid realizes that it's up to him to save
Leonard's skin. Wilder signals Sir Wilfrid's complete change-
of-heart by having him pull out a cigar and order Miss Plimsoll, of all people, to light it for him.

We next see the barrister's physicians busily preparing
him, against the express wishes of Miss Plimsoll, for the
strenuous weeks ahead: one is checking his blood pressure,
another prescribing pills. Meanwhile, the attorney for the

prosecution, Mr. Myers (Torin Thatcher), is questioning
Mrs. French's testy old housekeeper, Janet McKenzie (Una
O'Connor), about the night the murder took place. (Sir
Wilfrid has not arrived in court on time so the judge has
started the proceedings without him.) She testifies that
she heard screams in Mrs. French's bedroom on the night
in question, the particular evening when Leonard Vole usually called on Mrs. French. Furthermore, she says, after
Mrs. French's dead body was discovered, she found a bloody
kitchen knife--obviously stained with her mistress's blood.

When Sir Wilfrid finally arrives in court, he comes on
strong at once, throwing doubt upon McKenzie's theory about
the bloodstained knife by presenting evidence to show that
Leonard's blood, like Mrs. French's, is also type O; he could
have cut himself while using the knife for some other purpose.
Hence the bloodstains on his jacket--which Christine noticed
upon his arrival home--were not necessarily caused by contact with Mrs. French. Sir Wilfrid also questions the validity
of McKenzie's statement about the screams by cleverly lower-
ing his voice to test the range of her hearing. She protests,
admitting that she has for a long time been in need of a hearing aid but could never afford one. Therefore, he points
out, she couldn't have been certain what she heard. Furthermore, Sir Wilfrid insinuates that she made up the whole story
of her being present the night the murder took place out of
sheer revenge for Leonard's duping her of her share of Mrs.
French's will. The housekeeper, of course, denies this, but
her futile efforts to maintain a facade of dignity are all too
humorously apparent to the spectators.

Leonard's fate seems sealed when Christine appears
for the prosecution--although Sir Wilfrid is not terribly sur-
prised, as he had sensed her capacity for deception from the
start. She testifies that her stance is legitimate since she is
not legally married to Leonard; she was already married to a
man named Helm when she went through a ceremony with
Leonard in Hamburg while he was serving with the British
occupation forces after World War II. Furthermore, Christine
insists that Leonard came home on the night in question and
admitted to her that he'd murdered Mrs. French. Leonard
vehemently protests her statements, but his wife's testimony
appears more sincere to the jury members.

Sir Wilfrid refuses to give up despite all the evidence

incriminating Leonard and the harmful effects the proceedings
are having on his health. "My client is entitled to the best
that I can do--if that means taking pills to keep going, I'll
take one pill or two pills or all of them and the box as well,"
he declares. He remains skeptical of the validity of Christine's testimony despite the fact that Mr. Myers had warned
her of the penalties for committing perjury before she'd
given it. Just as he is racking his brain in vain trying to
formulate a new plan of attack, he receives a phone call
from a woman who says she has some revealing information
about Christine Vole. Sir Wilfrid and his assistant, Mayhew
(Henry Daniels), rush immediately to Euston Station, where
they encounter a Cockney trollop who bears a scar which,
she says, was inflicted by her former lover after Christine
Vole had stolen him away from her. "Wanna kiss me, ducky?"
she asks Sir Wilfrid, pulling back her hair to reveal the mark
under her ear. She has in her possession a collection of
love letters ostensibly written by Christine to a man named
Max, revealing Christine's plan to testify against Leonard in
an attempt to get him out of the way.

Charles Laughton and Elsa Lanchester.

The next day in court Sir Wilfrid uses the letters to
expose both Christine's plan involving Max and her penchant
for lying under oath. He calls her to the stand and gets
her to admit that she may have once known a man named
Max. Then, having hidden the actual letters, he holds up
a piece of paper with the wording of one of them on it and
reads the damaging statements. Christine denies having
written the letter, but then foolishly states that she writes
her letters not on white sheets like the one Sir Wilfrid is
holding but on small blue pieces of paper with her initials
on them. Sir Wilfrid, having coaxed her into identifying
her letter paper (he knew that if he had held up the real
letter at first she would have denied that it was hers and
he would have had to be satisfied with her statement), pulls
out the hidden leaflets and, immensely satisfied with the
success of his ploy, says with regard to the slip of paper
in his hand, "This happens to be a bill from my tailor for a
pair of extremely becoming Bermuda shorts." Watching from
the balcony, Miss Plimsoll declares proudly to everyone present, "That's what we call him--'Wilfrid the Fox.'" Earlier,
she had used this expression in a derogatory manner to describe her annoyance at his defiance of her authority. Wilder neatly recalls the phrase as a subtle means of implying
the growing camaraderie between the two.

Sir Wilfrid labels Christine a "chronic and habitual
liar" and suggests that all her past statements may be dis-
regarded as blatant perjuries. She lashes out at Leonard
in a desperate attempt to clear her name and nearly breaks
down in tears on the stand. Needless to say, the jury decides in favor of Leonard. However, there still exits in Sir
Wilfrid's mind a nagging suspicion regarding the facility of
the proceedings. He is not relieved, though; rather, he is
appalled to discover that his intuitions are correct: Christine enters the courtroom after the spectators have cleared
out and reveals that she and Leonard had been conspiring
together all along. He really had murdered Mrs. French in
order to collect the money left him in her will, and the two
of them had decided that the only way for Leonard to win
his case would be for Christine to speak for the prosecution
--and thereby risk imprisonment for perjury. The woman
whom Sir Wilfrid had met at Euston Station was none other
than Christine in disguise, and she had written the letters
herself as part of the plan. Sir Wilfrid is astonished that
he has unwittingly succeeded in freeing a murderer--and in

Sir Wilfrid arranges his pills in geometric patterns.

risking his health and principles in doing so. Then comes
a second twist in the plot: Leonard appears--no longer the
naive innocent but a scheming opportunist who snickers
smugly at the success of his plan--with a female acquaint-
ance, the person for whose sake he really went through
with the murder and the subsequent trial. Christine, suddenly realizing that he has had absolutely no concern for
her welfare, adds yet another twist to the already pretzel-
shaped plot by stabbing Leonard with the same knife he'd
used on Mrs. French. "She killed him," mutters Miss Plimsoll. "Correction--she executed him," Sir Wilfrid replies,
acknowledging both his sympathy for Christine's plight and
his decision to defend her against a murder charge. Miss
Plimsoll, now firmly on Sir Wilfrid's side, orders a nearby
attendant to cancel his trip to Bermuda, and the two of
them set off to prepare their case for the defense.

    Although this was an unusual film for Wilder in that it
was not an original story written directly for the screen, it

bears a remarkable resemblance to the bulk of his work,
both of the past and future. The various instances of deception, masquerade, verbal wit, multiple plot twists, and
free-for-all that occur in Witness look forward to the wild
farces which Wilder would later write with I.A.L. Diamond,
notably Some Like It Hot (1959), One, Two, Three (1961),
Irma La Douce (1963), and Kiss Me, Stupid (1964). More
specifically, the motif of a male loner (in this case Sir Wilfrid) being suddenly jolted out of his misanthropy by a
woman (here, Miss Plimsoll and Christine Vole) is reminiscent of Double Indemnity (1944), Stalag 17 (1953), and
Sabrina (1954) and looks forward to The Private Life of
Sherlock Holmes (1970) and Avanti! (1972).[1] Also, the
"parasitic oedipal relationship," as Stephen Farber labels
it, between the young fortune-hunter Leonard Vole and the
elderly widow Mrs. French closely resembles that between
Joe Gillis and Norma Desmond in Wilder's Sunset Boulevard
(1950), both of them "motivated by greed and pity, both
taking place in a house filled with mementoes of another
era, both ending in violence.[2]

There is also the typical Wilderean preoccupation with
habits and idiosyncrasies. For example, Sir Wilfrid is continually chastised for smoking by Miss Plimsoll: for many
years Wilder was a four-pack-a-day smoker, and self-
conscious references to the habit also appear in Sabrina
(1954), The Seven Year Itch (1955), Irma La Douce (1963),
and The Fortune Cookie (1966).[3] Sir Wilfrid's penchant for
testing his clients' honesty by reflecting the light from his
monacle in their eyes anticipates Schlemmer's heel-clicking
in One, Two, Three (1961) and Dino's unquenchable appe-
tite for good-looking women (he says he gets a headache if
he doesn't have sex every night) in Kiss Me, Stupid (1964).

And, of course, there is the typical Wilderean humor,
which serves two vital functions in the case of Witness.
First, it helps alleviate the tension of situations (Sir Wilfrid's interrogation of Leonard is interrupted frequently as
Sir Wilfrid searches for an inconspicuous place to hide his
cigar ashes). Secondly, it allows for variety in the courtroom scenes by drawing attention to detail (Sir Wilfrid arranging his blood-pressure pills in geometric patterns and

---

[Opposite:] Leonard panics as Christine (Marlene Dietrich)
appears as a witness for the prosecution.

removing them as the days of the trial pass; Miss Plimsoll's
wristwatch timer signaling--loudly--the hour for Sir Wilfrid's
next dose of medicine).

Wilder's method of transferring the play to the screen
does have its faults, however abundant its merits. His addition of two flashbacks, for example--one describing Leonard's growing relationship with Mrs. French and the other
his first encounter with Christine in a Hamburg cabaret--
merely serve to slow down the action, mainly because they
provide no further insight into character motivation but instead simply illustrate trivial events which could have been
neatly summed up in a few words by Leonard himself. They
are not needed to lend credibility to Leonard's story, for the
audience is already as sympathetic to his plight as is Sir
Wilfrid. The most logical reason for Wilder's inventing them
was to give the actress who plays Mrs. French (Norma Varden) extra lines.

Despite all of Wilder's efforts to leave his personal
stamp on the material, the film version of Witness for the
Prosecution remains essentially the whodunit which Christie
originally conceived--and this tends to dwarf the potential
impact of certain motifs which it shares with other courtroom films of the period. The main concern of the film, like
that of the play, is with the mechanics of plot and how they
contribute toward the building of suspense--the essentials of
a murder mystery. The material provides little room for
character study; we are only given insight into the motives
of the characters so far as they serve to wrap up every
possible loose end once the final denouement arrives. Consequently, although the viewer sympathizes with Sir Wilfrid
at the end when he realizes he's been duped, he is not, unlike in Anatomy of a Murder (1959), for example, invited to
reflect upon the ambiguous chain of events which have led
to this final ironic twist; an alternative is provided quickly
for Sir Wilfrid (the opportunity to defend Christine) in order to give the picture a happy ending of sorts. Also, the
battle between defense and prosecution is unevenly slanted
in favor of the former; the same problems recur in the later
I Want to Live! (1958) and Compulsion (1959). There is
really little excuse for such skimpiness here, since the atmosphere in the Old Bailey courthouse was not as formalized
as that of the Nuremberg one, where witnesses and attorneys were kept at a specified distance from each other

Billy Wilder relaxes with Arthur Hornblow, Jr., Laughton, and Dietrich on the set. (Photo courtesy of Museum of Modern Art/Film Stills Archive)

throughout the trials (see Judgment at Nuremberg, Chapter 7).

One does not really sense that Wilder's heart is in the project; this is clearly not Billy Wilder's Witness for the Prosecution, but rather Agatha Christie's Witness for the Prosecution adapted for the screen and directed by Billy Wilder. And as for the tribute to Hitchcock which Wilder intended it to be, his film lacks the ominous, almost tragic edge that pervades all of the Master's best suspense tales, most notably Vertigo (1958) and Psycho (1960). When Witness is all over, one is left with little more than the short-lived satisfaction of having been outwitted by an ingenious turn of events. Since its primary interest is to provide an audience with suspenseful drama and little else, the film remains a superficial entertainment. The employment of a

courtroom setting here is merely a situational convenience,
as was the use of a mansion as the central locale in Christie's And Then There Were None. The workings of the law
and the methods of its enforcers were not in the least the
main concern of the playwright, nor are they terribly important to Wilder as a scenarist. The fact that Witness has over
the years become probably the most popular and best-
remembered of all courtroom films attests to the low esteem
of the American movie-going public for drama which informs
as well as entertains.

One of the main factors contributing to its continued
popularity is undoubtedly the performances--Charles Laughton's masterful portrayal of Sir Wilfrid in particular. He
holds the whole film together; whether mugging through his
scenes with Miss Plimsoll or assuming the air of stately professionalism in the courtroom, he is a thorough delight. The
fact that he was in real life married to Elsa Lanchester lends
added credibility to their wonderfully comic nurse-patient
squabbles. Marlene Dietrich and Tyrone Power, however,
are something of a disappointment. Power gives a very unsubtle performance--he repeatedly shouts his wide-eyed
declarations of his innocence as though he were being cross-
examined by Perry Mason. Ironically, his ineptness in the
role works at the end by forcing the viewer to look at him
with disdain and at Christine with pity. As for Dietrich,
her intense eagerness to play the role is certainly not justified by her acting. While she is appropriately cold and cal-
culating as Christine, she shows remarkably bad taste in the
scene where she shouts at Leonard from the stand. However,
the character is basically only a cardboard one; the German
widow whom Dietrich portrays in Kramer's Judgment at
Nuremberg (1961) is a much more complex woman, and
Dietrich responds in kind with a characteristically dignified
performance. That her role in Witness has been regarded
by so many critics and fans as one of the highlights of
her career reveals only that they have very vague memories
of the film indeed. Una O'Connor, on the other hand, does
a beautifully comic turn as the greedy, pathetically funny
housekeeper.

This was Wilder's second collaboration with art director
Alexander Trauner and with accomplished editor Daniel Mandell, whose services he would again--and again--employ
throughout the next decade on The Apartment (1960), One,

Two, Three (1961), Irma La Douce (1963), Kiss Me, Stupid (1964), and The Fortune Cookie (1966).

All in all, Witness for the Prosecution, although a far cry from such elaborate explorations of the judicial process as Anatomy of a Murder (1959), remains the granddaddy of the countless courtroom-oriented gimmick suspense films of the 1930s and 1940s. Thanks to Wilder's flair for comedy and expertise at story-telling (he has repeatedly claimed that he is a writer first and foremost), the film doesn't dim a bit when compared to the impressive recent (1982) TV remake. Perhaps the greatest tribute to its success was made by Christie herself when, shortly before her death in 1967, she stated that Wilder's verion of her play was the best cinematic adaptation of any of her works.

NOTES

1. Steve Seidman, The Film Career of Billy Wilder (Pleasant-ville, N.Y.: Redgrave Publishing Company, 1977), p. 25.

2. Stephen Farber, "Billy Wilder," in American Directors, vol. 1 by Jean-Pierre Coursodon and Pierre Sauvage (New York: McGraw-Hill, 1983), p. 375.

3. Seidman, p. 20.

Chapter 3

I WANT TO LIVE!

Credits

A Figaro Production, released throug United Artists, 1958.
Producer: Walter Wanger. Director: Robert Wise. Screen-
play: Nelson Gidding and Don M. Mankiewicz, based on
newspaper articles of Ed Montgomery and the letters of
Barbara Graham. Music composed and conducted by John
Mandel. Jazz Combo: Gerry Mulligan, Shelly Manne, Red
Mitchell, Art Farmer, Frank Rosolino, Pete Jolly and Bud
Shank. Director of Photography: Lionel Lindon, A.S.C.
Editor: William Hornbeck, A.C.E. Art Director: Edward
Haworth. Set Director: Victor Gangelin. Costumers:
Wesley Jeffries, Angela Alexander. Makeup: Tom Tuttle,
Jack Stone. Hair Stylists: Emmy Eckhardt, Lillian Hokom
Ugrin. Script Supervisor: Stanley Scheuer. Production
Manager: Forrest E. Johnston. Assistant Director: George
Vieira. Sound: Fred Lau. Casting: Lynn Stalmaster.
Black-and-white. Running time: 120 minutes.

Cast: Susan Hayward (Barbara Graham), Simon Oakland
(Ed Montgomery), Virginia Vincent (Peg), Theodore Bikel
(Carl Palmberg), Wesley Lau (Henry Graham), Philip Coolidge
(Emmett Perkins), Lou Krugman (Jack Santo), James Phil-
brook (Bruce King), Bartlett Robinson (District Attorney),
Gage Clark (Richard G. Tibrow), Joe De Santis (Al Matthews),
John Marley (Father Devers), Raymond Bailey (San Quentin
Warden), Alice Backes (Barbara, San Quentin Nurse),

Gertrude Flynn (San Quentin Matron), Russell Thorson (San Quentin Sergeant), Dabbs Greer (San Quentin Captain), Stafford Repp (Sergeant), Gavin MacLeod (Lieutenant).

In addition to cinema adaptations of fictionalized trials, the 1950s and 1960s also saw the production of several films based on real-life cases, both of the past (the Leopold-Loeb case of the '20s in Compulsion [1959] and the Scopes Monkey Trial in Inherit the Wind [1960]) and of more recent years (the Nazi War Crimes trials in Judgment at Nuremberg [1961]).

One particularly sensational case of the 1950s concerned a 32-year-old woman named Barbara Graham, who was put to death in the gas chamber at San Quentin on June 3, 1955, for the alleged murder of Mrs. Mabel Monahan, an elderly Burbank widow. Graham had insisted to the end that she was innocent, and no one could be quite certain that she had indeed been guilty beyond a reasonable doubt, as her guilt had been to a large extent assumed on the basis of the facts of her illicit past (she had been arrested for soliciting, forgery, and narcotics abuse, among other things); no one actually saw her murder Mabel Monahan.

Intrigued by the dramatic potential of the Graham case, veteran producer Walter Wanger, who had been responsible for such well-received classics as John Ford's Stagecoach (1939) and Alfred Hitchcock's Foreign Correspondent (1940), decided that it would be ideal material for a motion picture. He thereupon hired Robert Wise to direct the new film. Wise, a highly versatile craftsman who had up to that time made films of considerable quality in several genres, including horror (The Curse of the Cat People [1944] and The Body Snatcher [1945] for Val Lewton), science fiction (The Day the Earth Stood Still [1951]) and film noir (The Set-Up [1949]), employed his usual practice of doing extensive research on the topic of his new film in order to heighten the realism of the piece. He was abetted largely by the efforts of Don Mankiewicz and Nelson Gidding, who based their scenario on newspaper and magazine articles by Pulitzer Prize winning journalist Edward S. Montgomery, who had become a close friend of Graham and had defended her in a series of articles for the San Francisco Examiner, the actual court transcripts, and Graham's personal letters written

Barbara (Susan Hayward) as the "goodtime girl."

during her term of imprisonment. (A note by Montgomery
himself which both precedes and follows the actual film attests to the factual basis for the screenplay.) Moreover,
Wise decided to shoot the film in a low-key, black-and-white
format in order to create a documentary style.

I Want to Live! is one of the only films of an actual
case whose characters retain the names of their real-life
counterparts. In Compulsion (1959), Clarence Darrow's
name is changed to Jonathan Wilk and those of Leopold and
Loeb to Judd Steiner and Artie Straus, respectively. In
Inherit the Wind (1960), Darrow is known as Henry Drummond,
William Jennings Bryan as Matthew Harrison Brady, H.L.
Mencken as E.K. Hornbeck, and John T. Scopes as Bertram T.

Cates. However, in both cases, the similarities to the real-
life figures are obvious enough, making the use of fictional
names seem an unnecessary intrusion. By not adhering to
convention in this respect, Gidding and Mankiewicz make it
all the more easy for the viewer to believe in the characters
in their screenplay right from the start.

The first half of I Want to Live! is characterized by a
staccato tempo in both cinematography and score (jazz) which
emphasizes the carefree lifestyle of "goodtime girl" Barbara
(Susan Hayward). We watch her peruse the seedy tenderloin
district of San Francisco as she participates in a number of
illegal activites (among them, prostitution, vagrancy, and
card sharking) by which she earns her daily bread and to
which she never gives even a second thought--that is, not
until her conspiring with two old "chums" named Sonny and
Mack lands her a five-year jail sentence for perjury.

After being released early on probation, Barbara re-
solves to create a decent life for herself. However, her
marriage to bartender Henry Graham (Wesley Lau) quickly
falters due to his growing dependence upon drugs. In spite
of this, though, Graham does succeed in providing her with
a son, who will remain her chief life-sustaining force throughout the story.

Unable to cope with stacks of unpaid bills and having
grown bored with the domestic life in general, Barbara becomes enthusiastic when she is asked by two crooks, Emmett
Perkins (Philip Coolidge) and Jack Santo (Lou Krugman), to
assist them in a series of petty crimes.

All goes well for the trio until they are arrested one
night for the alleged murder of Mrs. Mabel Monahan, a Burbank widow who was bludgeoned to death on the night of
March 9, 1953. An underground figure named Bruce King
(James Philbrook), who claims to have been present at the
scene of the crime, turns state's evidence and directs the
police to the hideout of Graham, Perkins, and Santo. The
actual crime is not shown to the audience; though word of
the murder had appeared in the headline of a newspaper
which had been lying outside Barbara's back porch and was
unnoticed by her (but not the viewer; Wise showed it plainly
in close-up), this is the first time the viewer is made aware
of its significance.

Barbara protects her son from her addict husband, Henry
Graham (Wesley Lau). (Photo courtesy of Museum of Modern
Art/Film Stills Archive)

Barbara in court with Tibrow (Gage Clark), Perkins (Philip
Coolidge), and Santo (Lou Krugman).

When Bruce King names Barbara as the actual killer,
she (despite her repeated pleas that she know nothing of
the whole incident) is promptly placed in a San Francisco
prison. Desperate for an out (her alibi of being home the
night of the murder can only be verified by her six-month-
old son and forgetful drug-addict husband) she agrees to
"buy" an alibi from a friend of one of her cellmates. But
the "friend" turns out to be a police officer who aids the
prosecution in getting a death penalty conviction by wran-
gling a phony confession out of her. By an ironic turn of
justice, Bruce King receives a promise of acquittal from the
D.A. and the prison sentence of Rita, Barbara's cellmate
who cooperated with the police, is reduced considerably.
Moreover, now that the case for the defense seems hopeless,
Barbara's weasel-like attorney, Richard G. Tibrow (Gage
Clark), requests an immediate withdrawal.

The second part of the film takes place at Corona,

the women's prison at San Quentin where Barbara lives out
the remaining agonizing days before her execution. Now the
frightening underlying implications of Barbara's activities
during the first part of the film are brought harshly to light
as the tempo of John Mandel's score becomes solemn, dirge-
ful (though employing the identical musical motifs which characterized the earlier section of the film).

Despite having been placed in solitary confinement,
Barbara loses none of her gutsy, rebellious spirit; she refuses to obey the prison's dress code ("I'll sleep raw") and
repeatedly refers (with a black humor that betrays her inner
fears) to the place as a college. "I'm a big girl on campus,"
she remarks, referring to the fact that she is the only woman
around who faces a death sentence.

As the days pass, a few people rally to Barbara's defense. Among them is her old friend Peg (Virginia Vincent),
who was once a partner in crime with Barbara but who has
"gone straight." It is Peg who arranges for Barbara to see
her little boy on a regular basis--the only relief that she is
permitted from the torture of solitude. Another important
individual is San Francisco Examiner reporter Ed Montgomery
(Simon Oakland), who gained considerable fame during the
trial for maligning Barbara in a series of articles in which
he labeled her "Bloody Babs." After interviewing her on
death row several times, however, he becomes increasingly
convinced of her innocence and writes a new batch of articles on her behalf. He becomes a close friend of hers during
her final days.

Another figure who makes a significant contribution to
the fight for Barbara's acquittal is psychiatrist Carl Palmberg (Theodore Bikel). After examining Barbara on several
occasions, he concludes that though she is admittedly totally
amoral and has no regard whatsoever for the law, she evinces
a distinct aversion to physical violence--and furthermore, he
notes that she could not possibly have murdered Mabel Monahan in accordance with Bruce King's testimony; he claimed
that Barbara had beaten Monaham with a club held in her
left hand, but Barbara is right-handed.

Things are beginning to look brighter for Barbara--
Carl has asked for an appeal, and it looks as though it will
indeed be granted--when he dies suddenly from a long-

Schoolchum Peg (Virginia Vincent) visits Barbara in prison.
(Photo courtesy of Museum of Modern Art/Film Stills Archive)

Robert Wise rehearses Hayward and Clark. (Photo courtesy
of Museum of Modern Art/Film Stills Archive)

standing heart condition. Carl was her last chance; in a
letter to Peg, she had described how completely she depended
upon his persistence. He was, she said, the only person
who really understood what she was going through. A final
blow comes when her petition to the Supreme Court is denied.

    Left with virtually no hope (although Montgomery
vows to try for new appeals) and with the date of execution
set for June 3, 1955, at 10 a.m., Barbara becomes more and
more fearful for the future of her son, whom she is no longer
permitted to see (there is a possibility that, following her
execution, he will become the property of the state). Her
spirit of defiance is gradually broken down, and her remaining days become almost unbearable. Her mental anguish
eventually reaches the point where she begins to look forward to her execution as a final catharsis. "Don't beg for
my life," she tells an earnest reporter. Bitterly mocking

the efforts of the staff to make her obey orders, she asks,
"What can anyone threaten me with now?" betraying her
realistic acceptance of the inevitable.

The staff does manage to remain sympathetic to her
plight (she gets the "royal treatment": fudge sundaes for
breakfast, etc.) but they are as helpless at the might of the
law as she is. "Wish we could give her the benefit of the
doubt," remarks an attendant as he solemnly performs his
task of preparing the deadly sulfuric acid-cyanide solution.
Wise makes this final segment of the film the most harrowing
of all as he pulls no punches in providing a cold, uncen-
sored look at every step that is taken in the routine process
of putting someone to death in the gas chamber. There are
grotesque close-ups of the black gloves worn by the attendants to protect their skin from the toxic cyanide eggs as they
remove them from a can. The gas chamber itself looms over
the death cell like a menacing creature from the deep.

As the clock ticks away the final minutes and Barbara
sits alone in her cell, her nerves shattered, the tension
reaches unbearable proportions. When a telephone rings,
the noise so startles a nurse that she drops the coffee tin
she was carrying, and it hits the floor with a resounding
crash. Wise provides enormous close-ups of the telephone
and clock in order to emphasize their special significance at
this point. Twice reprieves from the governor are granted
and just as quickly withdrawn. Finally, it looks as though
all hope is lost, and the march to the gas chamber begins.
Barbara asks for a mask to shield her eyes from the grue-
some parade of reporters who have gathered like so many
vultures around the chamber to watch her receive her final
comeuppance for a life devoted to crime. Barbara manages
nevertheless to retain a measure of dignity to the last, asking a nurse, "Are my seams straight?" Then, just as she
is about to step into the chamber, the telephone rings.
Barbara screams in anguish: "Why do they torture me?!"
The execution is temporarily postponed again. However, by
11:12 a.m., all maneuvers to save her having failed, the
final phone call comes, and at 11:34 a.m., the cyanide pel-
lets drop into the solution of sulfuric acid. Instead of focus-
ing on reaction shots of the spectators, Wise, much to the
viewer's surprise--and horror--allows his camera to observe
the gas filling the chamber and Barbara's clenched fist growing limp, signaling that it's all over. Outside, in the parking

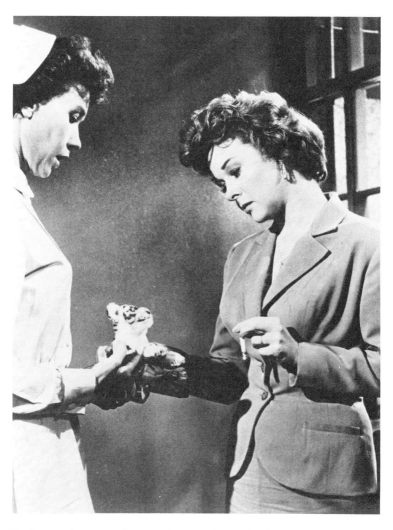

Barbara stares at her son's toy tiger during her last moments before execution.

lot, Ed Montgomery receives a letter: "Dear Mr. Montgomery
--I know you tried your best. I'm grateful. [Signed,]
Barbara Graham."

   To be sure, the ending of the film is a devastating
one; indeed so great is the viewer's indignation at the
forces which have contributed to this massive injustice that
he can well appreciate the logic behind the placing of an ex-
clamation point after the film's title. Thus I Want to Live!
ultimately takes the form of a fervent cry against capital
punishment--a more emotionally oriented one than that provided in the more downbeat 12 Angry Men and Compulsion.
However, it is precisely the picture's emotional pitch and
also the presence of Susan Hayward in the main part which
constitute the film's chief flaw, namely because they create a
presumption of innocence, even though Wise is not terribly
interested in Graham's guilt or innocence, and the viewer is
not given sufficient evidence to decide privately whether or
not she was guilty.[1] The reader will recall that we don't
actually see the murder take place. Wise sees Graham as a

Barbara is led to the gas chamber.

victim of circumstance, an unfortunate soul who, as a TV
announcer in the film so aptly puts it, "took the wrong fork
in the road of life." That Graham is doomed from the start
is foreshadowed by the credit title design: as the credits
progress, the I Want to Live! logo slowly fades into the background and eventually disappears. She is treated callously
throughout by the press and the representatives of law and
order simply because of her disreputable past. But Wise and
his screenwriters, Mankiewicz and Gidding, do not remain
resolutely attached to that view of Graham. They confuse
the issue of her presumed innocence with their indictment of
capital punishment by also raising the question, "Is capital
punishment wrong because of the possibility of judicial error, or because of the brutality of the police and their use
of informers?"[2] Indeed, the film would have been intellect-
ually more effective if Graham was guilty beyond doubt.
Wise's use of ambiguity (unlike Preminger's in Anatomy of
a Murder, for example) comes not as the result of a conscious desire on his part to make the audience decide for
itself exactly why capital punishment is wrong (although he
does hold that Graham was unjustly framed, which was not
actually the case), but rather as the result of an uneasy
attempt to subordinate all elements in the film to the Graham
character. Indeed, the casting of Susan Hayward in the
lead role had been foremost in Wise's mind from the start;
she had been chosen for the part by Wanger, her former
mentor, based on her proven (by three Academy Award
nominations) "heartbreak specialty" technique of acting in
biographical roles, such as in Walter Lang's With a Song
in My Heart (1952), where she portrayed crippled singer
Jane Froman, and in Daniel Mann's I'll Cry Tomorrow (1955),
in which she appeared as alcoholic star Lilian Roth. Wise
(who has repeatedly avoided making personal statements
on film in favor of advancing his commercial success) was
well aware of the impact that a single virtuoso performance
could produce at the box-office; Paul Newman's portrayal
of boxer Rocky Graziano in one of Wise's most recent films,
Somebody Up There Likes Me (1956), was a prime example.
This is not to say, however, that Susan Hayward's portrayal
of Barbara Graham is not a sincere and compelling one;
as an actress she is capable of eliciting much sympathy
from her audience--this despite the fact that "being a Hollywood star, she could hardly afford too realistic a portrayal
of the red-haired prostitute."[3] Any evaluation of I Want
to Live! is dependent to a great extent upon the viewer's

response to Hayward; at any rate, she was finally awarded
(and deservedly so) the Oscar that had eluded her three
times in the past.

The problem with Hayward's single standout performance is that Wise is so obsessed with it that ultimately it
becomes the single most memorable element in the film--
more important, even, than the denouncement of capital
punishment which is at the core of the drama and which is
put forth through the horror of the events which Graham
confronts. Wise chose the other members of his cast carefully, in order to ensure that their stature would not be a
threat to Hayward's. The resulting performances--by Virginia Vincent as Graham's loyal friend Peg (Vincent's face
has the essential honesty of Barbara Bel Geddes'), by Theodore Bikel as her devoted psychiatrist, Carl Palmberg, and,
finally, by Simon Oakland as Ed Montgomery (Oakland always
seemed to get typecast in similar roles; two years later
Hitchcock chose him to play the droll psychiatrist in Psycho
--are good, but so little attention is given to them (and this
includes Montgomery, whose real-life statements at the beginning and end of the film suggest that he will play a major part in the proceedings), compared to that which Hayward receives, that they seem almost bit parts. Another
qualm which the viewer might raise is why the director and
scenarists chose to spare no sympathy for Perkins and Santo,
Graham's accomplices, who, after all, shared the same fate
as she.

Reservations about the negative impact of the Hayward
performance aside, however, it must be said that it is one
of the film's major assets. Another is Wise's direction. He--
along with his scriptwriters--present their subject intelligent-
ly and honestly, although with an occasional tendency to go
overboard in the use of "streetwise" dialogue, particularly in
the case of the Graham character. Wise's own talents are especially evident in the chilling final segment in the gas chamber. And, as with every Wise film, from his Val Lewton
thrillers of the 1940s through his musicals of the 1960s, special emphasis is given to editing as a means of achieving dramatic tension. It is important to note in this context that
Wise began his career as editor of Orson Welles' masterpieces
Citizen Kane (1941) and The Magnificent Ambersons (1942).
In the case of I Want to Live!, he had at his disposal one of
the top cutters in the business, William Hornbeck. Although

Hornbeck had worked on Frank Capra's brilliant Why We
Fight documentaries back in the early forties, as well as
several other distinguished British (Rembrandt, The Four
Feathers) and American (The Heiress, A Place in the Sun,
Shane) productions, his skills had been demonstrated most
prominently two years before, in George Stevens' massive
3½-hour epic, Giant. Since Stevens' working procedure involved shooting a scene repeatedly (often as many as twenty
times) from various angles and viewpoints, the awesome task
of choosing the best takes from among thousands of feet of
footage lay in the hands of Hornbeck the editor. Indeed,
much of the credit for Stevens' Best Director Oscar for
Giant should go to Hornbeck. In Wise's film Hornbeck often
juxtaposes images to magnificently ironic effect: a shot of a
drum being pounded in a swinging nightclub where Graham
and company are planning yet another heist is followed by a
shot of a judge's gavel being banged on the bench as Barbara is sentenced to 5 years in jail for perjury. Barbara's
cry, "I've done nothing! Nothing, do you hear me?
NOTHING!" following her imprisonment for murder is continued by a TV newscaster reporting that "nothing" new has
developed in her case over the past several days.

Another indispensable asset to the documentary look of
the film that Wise was striving for is the skilled black-and-
white cinematography of Lionel Lindon. Lindon certainly
proved his versatility with this film: the low-key, unat-
tractively harsh look which he managed to create in this
instance was a far cry from the magnificent orange sunsets
of Mike Todd's Technicolor spectacular Around the World in
80 Days, for which Lindon had received an Oscar in 1956.
However, the atmosphere which he evoked for I Want to
Live! is perfect in keeping with the no-holds-barred, crusading approach of director Wise.

Also noteworthy is the jazz score of John (later to become "Johnny" of TV fame) Mandel, which alternates in tempo
from the first part of the film to the second, accelerating as
Graham initially plays the carefree goodtime girl, and slowing
down gradually as the atmosphere becomes more solemn and
ominous. It is interesting to note that jazz had become a
popular staple among motion pictures of the 1950s, beginning
with Elia Kazan's Streetcar Named Desire in 1951 (Alex North),
and continuing throughout the decade with Otto Preminger's
The Man with the Golden Arm (1955, Elmer Bernstein) and

Anatomy of a Murder (1959, Duke Ellington) and Orson Welles'
Touch of Evil (1958, Henry Mancini).

    Despite its many outstanding elements, however, I
Want to Live! is revived in theaters and on TV only infre-
quently. To be sure, its story is an unusually grim one;
one can understand why it has not become a popular entertainment among audiences (upon hearing the title, people
tend to recall the ghastly finale in the gas chamber, easily
the best segment in the film--thanks to Wise--but considerably unsettling). Audiences seem only to pay attention
to films of this nature when the outcome is positive (though
usually only superficially so, as in 12 Angry Men) or when
there is no message at all, just pure entertainment (Witness
for the Prosecution). However, perhaps it is better if view-
ers do not take I Want to Live! too seriously, for if they
accept the filmmakers' indictment of capital punishment,
they will then begin to believe that Barbara Graham was
indeed framed in real life, whereas her guilt was pretty
well established. There is no denying the credibility of
the complex portrait of this woman which Susan Hayward
provides us (and of which Lindsay Wagner's one-note portrayal of Graham in the 1983 TV remake of the film is only
a distant reminder). Nor can one dismiss Wise's devotion
to his subject (in interviews he frequently stresses the
considerable amount of research he did in preparation for
the filming), even though the impact of the final product is
somewhat marred by indecision, as mentioned earlier. Wise
remains to this day one of the industry's most flexible crafts-
men. Indeed, from viewing the harrowing final sequence of
I Want to Live! it is difficult, if not impossible, to believe
that it was directed by the same man who was responsible
for evoking the carefree spirit of The Sound of Music seven
years later. That he was able to execute both tasks with
such professionalism is an accomplishment in itself.

NOTES

1. Adam Garbicz and Jacek Klinowski, Cinema, the Magic
    Vehicle: A Guide to Its Achievement, vol. 2 (New York:
    Schocken Books, 1983), p. 409.

2. Garbicz and Klinowski, p. 410.

3. Garbicz and Klinowski, p. 410.

Chapter 4

COMPULSION

Credits

A Darryl F. Zanuck Production, released through 20th Century-Fox, 1959. Producer: Richard D. Zanuck. Director: Richard Fleischer. Screenplay: Richard Murphy, based on the novel and play by Meyer Levin. Music: Lionel Newman. Director of Photography: William C. Mellor, A.S.C. Editor: William Reynolds, A.C.E. Art Directors: Lyle R. Wheeler and Mark-Lee Kirk. Set Directors: Walter M. Scott and Eli Benneche. Wardrobe Design: Charles LeMaire. Costumes: Adele Palmer. Makeup: Ben Nye. Hairstyles: Helen Turpin. Assistant Director: Ben Kadish. Sound: Eugene Grossman and Harry M. Leonard. Orchestrations: Earle Hagen. Cinemascope lenses by Bausch and Lomb. Black-and-white. Running time: 103 minutes.

Cast: Orson Welles (Jonathan Wilk), Diane Varsi (Ruth Evans), Dean Stockwell (Judd Steiner), Bradford Dillman (Artie Straus), E.G. Marshall (D.A. Horn), Martin Milner (Sid Brooks), Richard Anderson (Max Steiner), Robert Simon (Lt. Johnson), Edward Binns (Tom Daly), Robert Burton (Mr. Straus), Wilton Graff (Mr. Steiner), Louise Lorimer (Mrs. Straus), Gavin MacLeod (Padua), Terry Becker (Benson), Russ Bender (Edgar Llewellyn), Gerry Lock (Emma), Harry Carter (Detective Davis), Simon Scott (Detective Brown), Voltaire Perkins (Judge).

The Leopold-Loeb murder case of the 1920s is one of the most infamous in history. Here are the details:

> On May 21, 1924, 19-year-old Nathan Leopold, Jr. and 18-year-old Richard Loeb (college students and homosexual lovers) murdered a 14-year-old boy named Robert Franks and planned to collect $10,000 ransom. But the body was discovered and States Attorney Crow broke down the alibi of the two young killers and brought them to trial. Criminal lawyer Clarence Darrow defended the boys. The young men were sentenced to life plus 99 years.

The possibility of creating a motion picture based on the events of the case remained slim for many years, mainly because it contained certain elements, such as homosexuality, which were considered taboo by the Motion Picture Production Code established in the United States in 1930. In 1948, when Alfred Hitchcock decided to base his first venture as independent producer, Rope, on the Patrick Hamilton play Rope's End, which was in turn based on the Leopold-Loeb case, he was forced to treat the honosexual relationship of the two protagonists so subtly that it was virtually nonexistent in the end product.

Fortunately, during the 1950s the restrictions of the Code were challenged openly with the release of three independently made productions. Otto Preminger's The Moon Is Blue (1953) introduced the words "virgin," "mistress," "pregnant," and "seduction" to the screen and his The Man with the Golden Arm (1955) gave a no-holds-barred look at the problems of a drug addict. The films were both released without the Code's Seal of Approval. One year later, in 1956, Elia Kazan's Baby Doll became the first motion picture of a major American studio (Warner Brothers) to be publicly condemned by the Catholic Legion of Decency, the organization responsible for establishing the Production Code in the first place. These three productions helped pave the way for a more explicit treatment of social and sexual themes in the cinema.

As a result of these changes, when, in the fall of 1956, Meyer Levin, a campus contemporary of Leopold and Loeb, published a best-selling novel based on their case and the

Domineering Artie (Bradford Dillman) threatens his partner
Judd (Dean Stockwell) after the latter slips up.

novel was turned into a Broadway play (which, unfortunately,
ran only 170 performances at the Ambassador Theatre in New
York), Darryl F. Zanuck, head of 20th Century-Fox, immediately jumped at the oppotunity to turn the play into a major
motion picture. However, Zanuck, at the time he purchased
the rights to the play (December 1957) was tied up in Africa
with The Roots of Heaven, directed by John Huston, so he
gave the Compulsion assignment to his 23-year-old son,
Richard.

     The plot of Compulsion follows closely the events of
the actual case. In 1924 Chicago, Artie Straus (Bradford
Dillman; prototype of Richard Loeb) and Judd Steiner (Dean
Stockwell; prototype of Nathan Leopold, Jr.) are law students at the University of Chicago. Both are 18, both are
sons of wealthy families, both are abnormally brilliant, and

both are strongly influenced by the philosophical writings of Nietzsche. Involved in a homosexual relationship underscored by tones of masochism and sadism, they decide to show their contempt for society and its laws by executing a perfect crime, one that is completely unemotional and purely the product of a superior intellect. After kidnapping 14-year-old Paulie Kessler, they murder him in the back seat of a rented car and pour acid on his body to conceal his identity (though none of this is shown to the audience) and dump his body in a culvert.

Their plan to collect ransom backfires, however, when the body is discovered and one of their fellow students, Sid Brooks (Martin Milner; prototype of Meyer Levin), a cub reporter for the Chicago Globe, visits the morgue and discovers that the boy did not drown, as reported, but was bludgeoned to death. Sid also uncovers a pair of eyeglasses that were found near the body. The police trace the glasses to, among others, Judd because of a specially-designed hinge,

Artie holding "Teddy." (Photo courtesy of UCLA film stills archive)

and he is questioned by District Attorney Horn (E.G. Marshall). He sticks to the alibi earlier agreed to with Artie, and although Horn calls in the latter to check the story, he is on the verge of letting them go when the Steiner family chauffeur arrives with an overnight case for Judd and inadvertently destroys the alibi.

By the time the brilliant lawyer Jonathan Wilk (Orson Welles; prototype of Clarence Darrow), an outspoken crusader against capital punishment, has been engaged to defend the pair, their guilt is established beyond all doubt (as indeed happened in the actual case, where the families thought the idea of their sons committing murder so preposterous that they did not engage Darrow until confessions had been obtained).

Rather than face a jury trial in a case in which public opinion has been raised to fever pitch, Wilk (who has already had a burning cross planted on his lawn by the local Ku Klux Klan) enters a plea of guilty, claiming that the boys, though not technically insane, were "sick" and could not be held entirely responsible. Horn counters by stating that there is "no other penalty but death" suitable in this case, for "never before has such a premeditated murder been committed." He has psychiatrists testify that Artie is a schizophrenic and Judd a victim of paranoia. Wilk concurs that indeed "their crime was most fiendish," but at the same time he defends their right to live by asking, "Isn't a lifetime behind bars enough for this mad act? Must this public be regaled with a hanging?" He points out that "never has there been a case in Chicago where under a plea of guilty a boy under 21 has been sentenced to death. Is it because their parents have money? I say that to deny the rich the same rights as the poor is to use the same type of thinking that started that fire" (he refers to the cross-burning on his lawn). He goes on to draw a clever parallel between the carefully calculated crime of Artie and Judd and that of "the officers of the state who for months have planned and schemed and contrived to take these boys' lives." Then, in what is perhaps the longest speech in film history (it runs for about fifteen minutes, without a single break), Wilk lashes out against capital punishment and all it stands for:

I've been fighting anger and hatred all my life. If

Judd attempts to rape Ruth (Diane Varsi) in a meadow.
(Photo courtesy of UCLA film stills archive)

there's one thing I've learned, it's that cruelty
only breeds cruelty. If there's any way of de-
stroying hatred, it's through love, charity and
understanding. I'm asking this court to shut these
boys in a prison for life. Any cry for more goes
back to the hyena.... Does anyone here know what
justice is? The world has been one long slaughter-
house from the beginning until today. Why not
think? Why not read something, instead of blindly
shouting for death? If our state is not kinder,
more considerate, more intelligent, than the mad
act of these two sick boys, then I'm sorry I've
lived so long.... Will killing these boys stop
further killings? No. Your honor, if you hang
these boys you turn back to the past. I'm pleading for the future. I'm pleading not just for these
two boys but for all boys, for all the young. I'm
pleading not just for these two lives but for life
itself, for a time when we can learn to overcome
hatred with love, when we can learn that all life is
worth saving, and that mercy is the highest attri-
bute of men. In this court of law, I'm pleading
for love.[1]

The next morning, the judge delivers his sentence:
life plus 99 years. Embittered, Judd and Artie scorn the
contention of Wilk, the renowned agnostic, that the outcome
was perhaps the will of God. Before the two are taken away,
Wilk leaves them with something to think about: "Sometime
you might ask yourselves whether it wasn't the hand of God
that dropped those glasses. And if He didn't, who did?"

The film version of Compulsion was scripted by Richard
Murphy, who had earlier written two excellent socially-
conscious, documentary-like dramas for Elia Kazan, Boomer-
ang! (1947) and Panic in the Streets (1950). Compulsion
marked a return to that genre, largely neglected throughout
the 1950s in favor of lighter fare, such as Billy Wilder's
Seven Year Itch (1955) and Witness for the Prosecution
(1958), Alfred Hitchcock's Rear Window (1954), To Catch a
Thief (1955), The Man Who Knew Too Much (1956), and
North by Northwest (1959) and, on a lesser note, the countless, mindless science fiction and horror flicks of the period.
Murphy's screenplay, although faithful to the play on which
it is based and to the details of the original case, is probably

the film's chief weakness. Pauline Kael accurately summed
up its shortcomings: "It can't make up its little bit of mind--
is it an exploration of thrills and decadence, or a piece of
crime research, or an attack upon capital punishment? There
are all kinds of possibilities in the material, but the movie
settles for all-purpose generalities."[2] Compulsion starts out
promisingly as a character study of two twisted young men,
but then becomes little more than a simple-minded detective
thriller when States Attorney Horn enters the picture, searching for clues and querying Straus and Steiner--and then
abandons both directions as it devotes its final half hour or
so to the courtroom sequence--which, apart from Wilk's ora-
tion, incidentally, has virtually no substance whatsoever.
There is no battle of wits between the prosecution and defense, because once Wilk begins his speech, everyone else--
including Horn--is reduced to silence. The circumstances surrounding the actual trial were a very different
story indeed: the prosecution summoned some eighty-two
witnesses to their side, and the defense, twenty-four![3]

Horn (E.G. Marshall) confronts Judd with evidence linking
him to the murder.

Wilk (Orson Welles) mocks one of Horn's ploys as the judge
(Voltaire Perkins) looks on.

As we have seen, a similar problem handicapped the earlier
I Want to Live!

    Richard Fleischer's direction, however, is a pretty
fair compensation for the script's rambling structure.
Fleischer was at the time a contract director for Fox who
had no discernable "personal signature" but who was a com-
petent craftsman, his best previous efforts having been in
the genres of suspense (The Narrow Margin, 1952) and adventure (Disney's 20,000 Leagues Under the Sea, 1954).
Compulsion marked his first assignment for Darryl Zanuck.
There are several scenes in Compulsion which, thanks to
Fleischer's flair for conveying the presence of menace without actually showing it--a technique he later perfected in
1968's Boston Strangler--come across as genuinely disturbing. For instance, the sequence preceding the credits--in

which Artie and Judd steal a typewriter and try to run down
a drunk encountered on the road home just for the fun of it
--is dimly lit, ominous, and frightening. Another example of
Fleischer's technique occurs in a scene in Judd's bedroom,
where Artie is berating him for "slipping up" with regard to
losing his glasses during the murder. Artie sits on a bed
trying to communicate his sense of disgust with Judd to a
teddy bear, asking it questions and nodding its head in
agreement. Fleischer inserts many off-center close-ups of
"Teddy," making the inanimate object seem to come alive and
thereby emphasizing the domineering, sadistic aspect of Artie.
It is a bizarrely amusing sequence on the surface, but unsettling in terms of its implications.

Still another notable scene occurs when Judd, in an
attempt at a second unemotional "thrill crime," takes Ruth
Evans (Diane Varsi), Sid Brooks' one-time girlfriend, out
to a meadow--ostensibly to enlist her aid in an ornithological
expedition, but in reality with the intent of raping her. The
background is made uncomfortably still and silent as Judd
moves toward Ruth and Fleischer cross-cuts between extreme
close-ups of her and Judd, both terrified of each other, until Judd, taken aback by Ruth's reply to his hopeful inquiry
as to whether she is afraid of him, "I'm afraid for you,
Judd," breaks down crying. "I'm so ashamed," he sobs
over and over. It is a quietly powerful moment, made all
the more eerie by the viewer's realization that the spot
where Ruth is sitting is the exact location where the murder
took place!

Despite Fleischer's often impressive handling of the
story, however (he has admitted that his favorite subjects
are murder cases, Compulsion topping the list), it is obvious that the application of Cinemascope, a special optical
process pioneered by Fox and used extensively throughout
the 1950s on Fox films, beginning with The Robe in 1953,
was unnecessary in this case. The Cinemascope system in-
volves the use of lenses that compress and distort images
during filming and spread them out undistorted during pro-
jection over an area wider than the normal motion picture
screen. The Cinemascope image, photographed on normal
35mm film, is about $2\frac{1}{2}$ times as wide as it is high when it is
projected, an aspect ratio of 2.35:1, as compared with the
conventional screen aspect ratio of 1.33:1. Since Compulsion
was a small-scale, black-and-white drama, not a wide-screen

Technicolor extravaganza, distortion of the image was not
needed--although Fleischer handles the process competently
enough; this is not surprising when one considers that he
had already worked with Cinemascope successfully six times
before, on 20,000 Leagues Under the Sea (1954), Violent Saturday (1955), The Girl in the Red Velvet Swing (1955),
Bandido (1956), Between Heaven and Hell (1956), and
These Thousand Hills (1959).

   What distinguishes Compulsion most of all are probably
the performances--that of Orson Welles as Wilk (Darrow) in
particular. In order to look properly worn-out and bloated
for the role, Welles' hairline was shaved, his hair dyed, his
body padded, and latex bags were placed under his eyes.
As he does not appear until the last third of the film, his
is almost a guest appearance, but his presence becomes the
most memorable in the production. His portrayal of Darrow is
his characteristically flamboyant one, though he lends an admirable restraint and inner conviction to the role (indeed,
so much so that, as Variety's critic noted, "The lines he

Diane Varsi and Orson Welles.

Wilk makes his eloquent plea for "love, charity and understanding." (Photo courtesy of UCLA film stills archive)

speaks become part of the man himself"[4]). For Welles, the
Darrow character was the direct antithesis of the corrupt
detective whom he had played the year before in his own
thriller, Touch of Evil. His Darrow is perhaps a bit more
dog-tired and less fiesty than Spencer Tracy's in Inherit
the Wind (1960), but it is equally compelling in its own
way, and it is illuminating the compare the two portrayals.

Bradford Dillman's Artie is an intensely chilling mas-
termind, the dominant partner in the homosexual relationship.
Dean Stockwell's Judd is a more subtle characterization,
a wealth of repressed fears and anxieties concealed beneath
a facade of intellectual superiority. All three actors shared
the Best Actor award at the Cannes Film Festival for their
performances. E.G. Marshall's Horn is cunning and clever,
but decidedly one-dimensional--but that is the fault of the
script, not the actor. Diane Varsi, then a newcomer to

films, was adequate as the girl who fears but understands
and wants to help Judd.

Darryl Zanuck had originally planned to get a real
judge for the courtroom sequence, but failed (Otto Preminger, it will be seen, was the only producer who succeeded
in doing so; he convinced Joseph N. Welch, the Boston
attorney-turned-judge who condemned Joseph McCarthy,
to play the judge in Anatomy of a Murder [1959]). However, the actor who was given the part, Voltaire Perkins,
proved to be an inspired choice nevertheless; not only was
he an ex-lawyer and one-time pro tem judge, but also a
personal friend of Clarence Darrow and his guest at the
original Leopold-Loeb trial. Unfortunately, unlike Judge
Welch in Anatomy, Perkins was scarcely heard from at all
during the course of the courtroom sequence in Compulsion.

The film's release in early 1959 was beset by controversy. In March 1958, Nathan Leopold, Jr. had been
paroled--at age 53--from Stateville Prison and was doing
medical research in Puerto Rico for $10 a month at a Church
of the Brethren field hospital. In October 1959 he filed suit
against 20th Century-Fox for $1.5 million in damages on the
grounds that Meyer Levin had appropriated his name, like-
ness and personality for profit. Nothing came of it,
though, as it was discovered that audiences liked the film
made from Levin's play. Altogether, Compulsion grossed
about $1.5 million on its initial release. Incidentally, Leo-
pold died in 1971 at age 66 of a heart ailment. He was still
living in Puerto Rico at the time. Loeb had been slain in a
razor fight reportedly prompted by a homosexual assault in
1936 in Stateville Prison.

Today Compulsion remains an earnest, intelligent, solid
depiction of the Leopold-Loeb case, worthwhile mainly for Orson Welles' eloquent portrayal of Darrow and for the fine
period atmosphere which its director, Fleischer, managed to
evoke. Unfortunately, the reteaming of Zanuck (as producer-
screenwriter this time), Fleischer, cameraman William Mellor,
and stars Welles and Dillman the following year for a similar
courtroom-oriented thriller, Crack in the Mirror, produced
no more than a thudding bore. Although it sticks to the
facts of its historical source somewhat better than did the
earlier I Want to Live!, it too is marred somewhat by an in-
decisive screenplay. Also, like I Want to Live!, it tends to

subordinate the supporting roles in the cast rather uneasily
to those of its leads. Both films remain inferior to Anatomy
of a Murder, the subject of the next chapter in this book,
in that they do not manage to leaven the unpleasantness
of their subject matter with comedy. But then some subjects warrant a heavier treatment than others. Such appears to be the case with Compulsion, which is a relent-
lessly serious tale.

NOTES

1. Richard Murphy, Unpublished screenplay for Compulsion,
    (20th Century-Fox, 1959).

2. Pauline Kael, article on Compulsion in 5001 Nights at the
    Movies (New York: Holt, Rinehart and Winston, 1982),
    p. 119.

3. Lesley Oelsner, article on death of Nathan Leopold, Jr.
    in New York Times, August 31, 1971, p. 65.

4. "Hift," review of Compulsion in Variety, February 4,
    1959.

Chapter 5

ANATOMY OF A MURDER

Credits

A Carlyle Production, released through Columbia Pictures, 1959. Producer and Director: Otto Preminger. Screenplay: Wendell Mayes, from the novel by Robert Traver. Director of Photography: Sam Leavitt, A.S.C. Editor: Louis R. Loeffler, A.C.E. Production Designer: Boris Leven. Music: Duke Ellington. Set Decoration: Howard Bristol. Makeup: Del Armstrong and Harry Ray. Wardrobe: Michael Harte and Vou Lee Giokaris. Sound: Jack Solomon. Sound Effects: Don Hall. Hairstyles: Myrl Stoltz. Music Editor: Richard Carruth. Key Grip: Leo McCreary. Lighting Technician: James Alquirst. Camera Operator: Irving Rosenberg. Script Supervisor: Kathleen Fagan. Costume Coordinator: Hope Bryce. Production Manager: Henry Weinberger. Assistant to the Producer: Max Slater. Assistant Director: David Silver. Titles: Saul Bass. Black-and-white. Running time: 160 minutes.

Cast: James Stewart (Paul Biegler), Lee Remick (Laura Manion), Ben Gazzara (Lt. Frederick Manion), Arthur O'Connell (Parnell McCarthy), Eve Arden (Maida), Kathryn Grant (Mary Pilant), Joseph N. Welch (Judge Weaver), Brooks West (Mitch Lodwick), George C. Scott (Claude Dancer), Murray Hamilton (Alphonse Paquette), Orson Bean (Dr. Smith), Alexander Campbell (Dr. Harcourt), Joseph Kearns (Burke), Russ Brown (Lemon), Howard McNear (Dr.

Dompierre), Ned Weaver (Dr. Raschid), Jimmy Conlin (Madigan), Ken Lynch (Sgt. Durgo), Don Ross (Duane Miller), Lloyd Le Vasseur (Court Clerk), Royal Beal (Sheriff Battisfore), John Qualen (Sulo), James Waters (Army Sergeant), Duke Ellington (Pie-Eye).

According to Michigan Supreme Court Justice John D. Voelker, the whole story began

> one chilly fall election day [back in 1955 when], after serving for 14 years as district attorney of the ... county [of Marquette] where I was born ... I found myself abruptly paroled from my job by the unappealable verdict of the electorate. The thing was almost painless: a few punches and pulls of the "wrong" voting gadgets and--presto--I was an ex-D.A.
>
> I also found myself in a bit of a bind. I was fast approaching fifty, two of our three daughters were in college, and between prosecuting criminal cases and pursuing the elusive trout, it seemed I had neglected anything as mundane as building up a private law practice....
>
> For a spell I tried various stratagems to avoid all those lurking aforesaids.... I wrote my second book about my D.A. experiences, which was duly accepted and published and generously reviewed but which nevertheless raced the first one--along with an interim book of short stories--to a blissful out-of-print oblivion, where all three still slumber.
>
> By then another election year had rolled around, so I threw my hat in the ring for Congress (a fate common to unemployed ex-D.A.s, I have since observed), but I barely carried my own county in our sprawling northern Michigan district.
>
> Since neither ... spinning yarns nor free trips to Washington seemed to be in the cards, I pondered my next move on how I might duck those pesky aforesaids.
>
> Then a rare intruding client interrupted my meditations, an aggrieved citizen who, it seemed, had inadvertently sneezed while rounding a highway curve and had been picked up by the cops for drunk driving. Would I defend him against this

crass miscarriage of justice? I would and did, and
though I forget just how justice fared in that one,
I soon began popping up in scattered justice courts
defending similarly aggrieved citizens.

Then a series of felonies began sweeping the
county, like an invasion of locusts, and, apparently
since I hadn't quite lost the courthouse and jail
during my D.A. stint, I suddenly found myself up
to my ears acting as defense counsel down in the
old stone courthouse overlooking Lake Superior.

When the approach of winter came a lull in the
crime wave, and I briefly considered writing a deep
think-tank piece--complete with both footnotes AND
footpads--on the eerie effects of changing seasons
on human behavior.

I already had the title: "Weather to Steal or
Not to Steal." Instead I had a sudden impulse to
write my first novel. After all, I reflected, I'd
already written books of yarns, so why not for a
change tackle and concentrate on one single story,
say, about one single courtroom trial?

Since I now bore the scars of fighting on both
sides of the courtroom barricades, I finally decided
to write about a murder trial. The courtroom was
one arena I knew about, and by now I'd appeared
on both sides in some pretty bang-up murder trials.

About then I recalled the farewell words of the
teacher of the only creative writing course I'd ever
taken. "Remember, kids," the man had said, "writing about people and places you know can help give
your stuff the ring of authenticity." He paused
and smiled. "And never forget that old saying:
'An ounce of authenticity is worth a pound of
windgassity.'"

Another reason I wanted to tackle a single
courtroom trial was that I had a small ax of my own
to grind. For a long time I had seen too many movies and read too many books and plays about trials
that were almost comically phony and overdone,
mostly in their extravagant efforts to overdramatize
an already inherently dramatic human situation.

I longed to try my hand at telling about a criminal trial the way it really was, and, after my years
of immersion, I felt equally strongly that a great
part of the tension and drama of any major felony

trial lay in its very understatement, its pent and
almost stifled quality, not in the usually portrayed
shoutings and stompings and assorted finger-
waggings that almost inevitably accompanied the
sudden appearance of that monotonously dependable
last-minute witness....

In what other forum, I asked myself, could a
battle for such awesomely high stakes--freedom and
sometimes life itself--be fought in such a muted atmosphere of hushed ritual and controlled decorum,
one so awash with rhetorical antiquities as "If it
please Your Honor" and all the rest?

So I scribbled the winter away, doggedly ex-
punging all aforesaids, finally putting down my pen
and taking up my fly rod and bundling my story
off to the New York publisher of my last book.
Then I folded my arms and impatiently awaited his
ecstatic response. One day it came, puzzlingly
accompanied by my manuscript, of all things....

Rallying, I tried another New York house and
once again waited for courtroom authenticity to
prevail. Prevail it did not, but instead my manuscript, along with a terse mimeographed rejection
slip, almost beat me back from the post office, at
least establishing a new speed record in my mount-
ing collection of rejections.

Then one evening while I was out fishing,
amidst the hum of insects and the swoop of night-
hawks, I suddenly remembered an editor who'd
worked on my last book and liked it. So the next
morning, almost apologetically, I baled the manuscript of Anatomy of a Murder off to Sherman Baker
at the New York house where he worked and--
presto--both he and St. Martin's grabbed it--and
doubtless saved me from a lifetime bondage to said
aforesaids.[1]

And from poverty, Anatomy of a Murder, which Voelker wrote
under the pseudonym of Robert Traver, immediately became a
bestseller--and stayed one for a record 61 consecutive weeks!

It was inevitable that Hollywood would eventually get
word of such an overwhelming success. It did so in the form
of Otto Preminger, one of the forerunners of the independent
producers, who had come to prominence following the collapse

Arthur O'Connell and James Stewart in <u>Anatomy of a Murder</u>.

of the Hollywood studio system in the late 1940s and early
1950s, the result of the interference of televison and other
factors with the entertainment interests of the American
public. The studios by now had "abandoned their old
assembly-line production of 'A' and 'B' pictures and [had
become], in the main, landlords, financiers and distributors
of film."[2] Thus, although the independent filmmaker had
secured "freedom from the domination of the production execu-
tives of old ... his now [were] all the choices which were
once made by vice-presidents in charge of production, associate producers, story departments, casting directors, even
costume designers."[3] In addition, since Americans now had
a choice of whether to entertain themselves with TV (which
was free) or to pay to see a motion picture, they had become
much more picky with regard to the latter. Gone were the
days when the name of a major star alone would secure fi-
nancial success for a film. By the mid-1950s

> there [was] not one star in the entire industry who
> [had] not appeared in a flop....
> [The] shift of emphasis from star to story [led]
> to a grimly competitive quest for film properties
> strong enough in potential popular appeal to justify
> the inflated cost of movie-making. It ... also led
> to a greater emphasis on the "pre-sold" property--
> one which has proved its worth as a best-selling
> book or hit play....
> Hollywood's "new man," the independent produc-
> er, if he [was] to survive, [had to] be a front
> runner in the race for outstanding properties.[4]

Such a man was Otto Preminger, the ultimate autocrat,
often ruthless and arrogant but always fiercely determined
to get what he wanted no matter what the price. He had
aroused one of the most heated controversies in Hollywood
history when, in 1953, he released his Moon Is Blue--which
contained such words as "virgin," which had never before
been uttered on the screen--without the seal of approval of
the Production Code. In a similar fashion, his Man with the
Golden Arm, made two years later, also set a precedent by
becoming the first Hollywood film to deal openly with a for-
merly taboo subject: drug addiction. It too was released
without the Production Code's approval. Both of these films,
incidentally, were also directed by Preminger.

James Stewart and Lee Remick: the interview. (Photo
courtesy of UCLA film stills archive)

It was understandable, therefore, that Preminger
would be attracted to the Traver novel, which dealt in explicit detail with such sensational issues as murder and rape.
Such topics spelled p-u-b-l-i-c-i-t-y to the independent producer eager for a commercial success that would enable him
to continue searching for new properties. Indeed, this was
certainly on Preminger's mind at the time, for two of his latest
features, Saint Joan (1957) and Bonjour Tristesse (1958),
had been disasters at the box office.

But perhaps more important, what intrigued Preminger
about Traver's book was the fact that "its intense reality
and its vivid picture of the law reminded him of his own days
as a law student."[5] Indeed, four of his previous films--Laura
(1944), Fallen Angel (1945), The Court Martial of Billy Mitchell (1955), and Saint Joan (1957) had all dwelled to some de-
gree on courtroom proceedings.

At any rate, Preminger completed the purchase of the film rights to <u>Anatomy</u> in July 1958.[6] His next step was to get a script out of the 437-page novel. He passed up the big name Hollywood writers and chose an unknown named Wendell Mayes, who had only written one screenplay previously--<u>The Spirit of St. Louis</u> (1957)--in collaboration with Billy Wilder, who recommended him to Preminger.

Preminger's quest for realism in both story and setting for his film of <u>Anatomy</u> turned out to be just as strong as that which had motivated Traver to write his novel in the first place. When Nat Rudich, a member of his publicity staff, suggested that Preminger get a real judge for the trial scenes after Spencer Tracy and Burl Ives had both turned down the role,[7] Preminger was highly intrigued: after all, this had never been done before, and if he could indeed get a real judge, it would add immeasurable commercial value to the picture. Rudich suggested the name of Joseph N. Welch, the Boston lawyer who had represented the Army during the McCarthy Senate hearings and had uttered the condemnation of the late senator: "Have you no sense of decency, sir?" Welch had later become a judge. Preminger immediately telephoned Welch at his home in Boston.

Parnell McCarthy (Arthur O'Connell) agrees to take the case.

At first, Welch was reluctant to comply, having been reminded, most likely, as Traver had been, of the countless
melodramatic Hollywood-version courtroom productions that
very nearly made a mockery of the law. However, as Preminger's friend Willi Frischauer recalls,

> Preminger's dedication to authenticity made a strong
> impression [on Welch]. His knowledge of the law
> and legal procedure was profound. That the author
> of the book was an eminent legal personality was an-
> other incentive.... Welch promised to think it over,
> but his friend Ed Murrow and others advised against
> --it might well dilute the public conception of him as
> a distinguished national personality.
>   Welch was not bothered. "What are the hours I
> would have to work?" he asked Preminger. "Nine
> to five," was the answer. "What would my wife be
> doing all this time?" "I have an idea," Preminger
> said. "She can join the cast and play a member of
> the jury." That decided it.[8]

So Anatomy of a Murder became the only courtroom film in
history to have a real judge play a fictional one.

   Even more important than the casting of Welch to the
realistic aspect of the production was the choice of setting.
Since many of the events depicted in the novel were taken
directly from actual experiences of the author, Preminger
decided, upon first glimpsing the Upper Peninsula communities of Ishpeming and Marquette during a visit to Traver's
home in the spring of 1958, to shoot the exteriors on location there. However, following a second trek to the Upper
Peninsula in January 1959, he decided to shoot the entire
film there (a procedure theretofore unheard of in film making). According to film historian Richard Griffith,

> This was partly due to his art director, Boris Leven,
> who felt that the peculiar provincial individuality of
> the area could not be recreated on a studio set. But
> other considerations had been gathering weight in
> the producer's mind. "It's not only the look of the
> place that I want to get on the screen. I want the
> actors to feel it, to absorb a sense of what it's like
> to live here--to smell it. In a Hollywood-made pic-
> ture, even when you shoot exteriors on location, the

core of the film is the studio-made scenes; the exteriors are just hung on to achieve a surface realism. But Anatomy is a story which requires reality.
I'm going to bring the whole cast [including James
Stewart, Lee Remick, Ben Gazzara, Arthur O'Connell and George C. Scott] and crew [Sam Leavitt,
his cameraman on three previous films; Lou Loeffler,
the editor of every Preminger film since Laura in
1944; among others] up here and install them in
Ishpeming. We'll live through it together and that
will help to make the film more 'real' than any single
thing I could do."

Judge Voelker was pleased. He had already been
asked to be a technical adviser for the courtroom
scenes of the picture [along with Judge Welch.]
Now he could do his advising on his home ground,
where his suggestions could be expected to prevail.

And so the fictional town of Iron City in Anatomy of a Murder [became] a composite of the actual
towns of Ishpeming and Marquette, Michigan. The
courtroom, jail and hospital scenes were shot in
their actual counterparts in Marquette, while the
scenes in the law library, at the railroad station,
and the opening scene of a small bar, were done in
Ishpeming. Paul Biegler's (James Stewart's) law
office [was] Judge Voelker's actual law office in
Ishpeming, situated in the house in which he was
born.[9]

In addition, Preminger cast actual members of the Marquette
and Ishpeming communities as spectators in the courtroom
scenes. Of course, the arrival of the "movie people" generated much excitement among the local townsfolk, but no
one was as overwhelmed by the festivities as Judge Voelker,
who soon found himself "as helplessly enmeshed and movie-
struck as a Cherry Queen.... For a writer of a book to
behold famous and talented people like Joseph N. Welch [who
later became a close friend], James Stewart, and lovely Lee
Remick and all the others of this superb cast toiling over
the very same words he but so lately toiled over himself in
his writer's solitude is simply an indescribable experience."[10]

Aside from the unusual facts surrounding its production, however, Anatomy of a Murder remains unique among
the other courtroom films of its time because of the nature

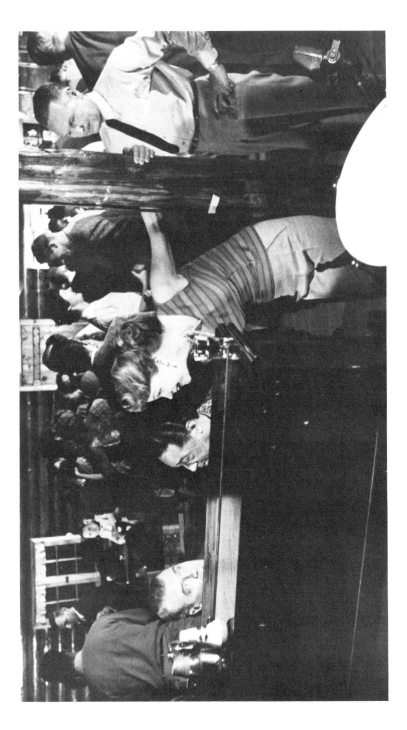

of presentation of its story. This is not a whodunit in which
all other elements are subordinated to the mechanics of plot,
but rather a character study of a group of people who, by
dint of sweet chance, have found themselves implicated in
the events surrounding a trial involving such sordid issues
as rape and murder. Hence, since we are dealing with real
people and not caricatures or stereotypes, the question of
motives becomes a primary concern. Human beings, after
all, are not perfect, and their propensities for telling their
own version of the truth of a story (usually with the intent
of deliberately misleading others in order to achieve a goal)
are here laid bare. As Garbicz and Klinowski point out,
"People are, in Anatomy, shown to be unfathomable and con-
tradictory, their motives as highly ambivalent, and the mood
is one of disenchantment and equivocation.... The point is
that [here] ambiguity becomes institutional."[11] Indeed, that
last statement more than any other accounted for Preminger's
attraction to the story in the first place; as he put it, "You
never know the truth." Because of the presence of shady
types and also because the film contains no flashbacks to
what actually happened--as in an actual murder case--there
must be one figure in the scheme of things with whom the
audience can identify as it tries to separate fact from fiction.

    This person turns out to be small-town attorney Paul
Biegler (James Stewart). As the film opens, Biegler is asked
to act as defense counsel for an army lieutenant accused of
murdering the man who allegedly raped his wife. Biegler,
who was recently defeated for re-election as public prosecutor of the county of Iron Cliffs, has all but abandoned his
law practice in order to pursue his favorite pastime, fishing.
His old friend, a drunken, has-been lawyer named Parnell
McCarthy (Arthur O'Connell), sees in the case of the lieutenant a chance for Paul to recoup his old enthusiasm for
fighting for justice--and, through Paul's efforts, one last
opportunity for Parnell to pull himself together by assisting
him. After Paul's secretary, Maida (Eve Arden) reminds
him of the stack of unpaid bills which his laziness has in-
curred, he agrees to at least look into the case.

    He is soon introduced to Lt. Frederick Manion (Ben

[Opposite:] Laura (Lee Remick) flirts at a local roadhouse.
Stewart and Ellington are at the piano.

In court, Paul fashions fish hooks to help him think. (Photo
courtesy of UCLA film stills archive)

Gazzara), who presents himself as a moody, enigmatic, hostile sort. Manion tells Biegler that on the night in question
his wife Laura came home late to their trailer, badly bruised,
with the news that she had just been raped by Barney Quill,
the owner of a nearby tavern. Manion says he immediately
proceeded to Quill's bar, where he shot Quill three times in
the chest, "causing," as Parnell had quipped earlier, "Quill
to promptly die of lead poisoning."[12] Manion is confident
that he will be able to get out of jail under the "unwritten
law," according to which, he says, he was justified in shooting Quill because Quill had violated his property (his wife).
Biegler promptly informs Manion that "the unwritten law is a
myth--it doesn't exist--and anyone who commits a murder on
the theory that it does exist has just bought himself room
and board in the state penitentiary--probably for life." He
further informs Manion that his situation doesn't fit into any
of the four most common methods for defending murder:

1) It was suicide or accidental; 2) It was self-defense; 3) The
killing was excusable; 4) The killing was legally justified.
The fourth defense does not qualify in this case because a
full hour elapsed between the time Manion's wife stumbled
into their trailer with her story and Manion's arrival at Quill's
bar. This worries Biegler. "Manion could have phoned the
police or asked the trailer park attendant for help--why
didn't he?" the lawyer wonders. (This sequence, titled "The
Lecture," in which Biegler coaches Manion as to the best defense strategy for him, aroused the indignation of many real-
life attorneys, who felt that it presented them in an unfavorable light.)

At this point, Biegler is not certain whether he wants
to take the case; in fact, he is leaning more toward the negative, as he tells Parnell: "I'm not the right attorney for
this fella--he's insolent, hostile...." However, before making
a decision he interviews Manion's wife, Laura (Lee Remick),
who, he discovers, is a sexpot and unabashed flirt--she is
even seductive toward him. She basically supports her husband's story, adding that she had agreed to let Barney Quill
drive her home because she had been frightened by his remark that bears roam the woods at night, and that, once
they were alone, he took advantage of her and beat her
when she tried to resist. When Biegler informs her of a
medical examiner's statement that he found no physical evidence of rape on her body, she insists that the man is
wrong ("A woman doesn't mistake these things"). Biegler
also manages to trap her on a couple of minor inconsisten-
cies in her story, but is uncertain (as is the viewer) of
their significance in determining the validity of her tale.
Incidentally, though Laura's story features some highly dis-
tasteful descriptions, this scene contains a great deal of humor, derived mostly from Biegler's growing uneasiness with
her continual references to her sexuality:

> Biegler: Doesn't a woman sort of instinctively know
> when a fella's on the make?
>
> Laura: Oh, sure. But that's only usual with me.
> With men, I mean. All men, ever since I was a
> kid. You, for instance. You're interested, but
> there isn't any reason to be afraid of you. It
> was like that with Barney.
>
> Biegler (somewhat taken aback): Now, Mrs. Manion--

Preminger lines up a shot while Joseph Welch, Murray Hamilton, and Brooks West listen to instructions. (Photo courtesy of UCLA film stills archive)

Laura (pleading): Call me Laura.

Biegler: Laura, I can assure you, I'm only interested in defending your husband. Nothing more....

Laura: Oh, I don't mean you'd try anything. It's ... it's the way you look at me.

Biegler: Well, it would be very difficult not to look at you.

Laura: The way I dress, you mean? You don't like it?

Biegler (unconsciously): Oh, I love it, I just ... (regaining an authoritative stance). Now, we'd better keep moving, here....

(later):

Biegler: Now, what were you wearing that night?

Laura (playfully):   You mean underneath?   A slip,
panties and a bra.

Biegler: No girdle?

Laura: No, no girdle.   I don't wear a girdle.   Do
you think I need a girdle?

Biegler (flustered):   I don't know....   Look, I'm
only interested in getting some facts that will be
of help in the defense of your husband, nothing
more....

Biegler further discovers that Manion is insanely jealous of his wife, who has gained a reputation for giving her
favors to other men.   Finally, against his better judgment
and mainly out of concern for his depleted bank account,
the attorney decides to accept the case.

But the lieutenant tells him that he is not able to provide him with half the fee up front, and that even if Biegler
is able to win his case for him he will have to give him a
promissory note for most of the amount.   So why does Paul
decide to take the case?   We discover that even his actions
are governed by personal motives: for one thing, he sees a
chance to beat Mitch Lodwick (Brooks West), the prosecutor
of the case and the man who recently defeated him in the
race for public prosecutor.   For another, he is convinced
that the ancient principles of Justice are still worth fighting
for (even if justice itself cannot always be guaranteed).
However, unlike the motives of Manion--who is anxious to
save his skin--and of Laura--who may be deliberately per-
juring herself to help him and also to conceal from him the
fact that she was not raped--Paul's motives are not so selfish that they could alter the outcome of the trial.   Once he
takes the case, Beigler remains thoroughly devoted to his
clients and is willing to overlook the fact that they may be
lying to him.   He manages to get Parnell to stop drinking
temporarily so that he will be able to assist him in court
and also makes Laura strop frequenting roadhouses with
other men.

He finds rounding up sympathetic witnesses easier
said than done, however.   The bartender at Quill's place,

Alphonse Paquette (Murray Hamilton), is a disagreeable type
who was a loyal friend of Quill and who appears to be covering up for the manager of the Thunder Bay Inn, a young
woman named Mary Pilant (Kathryn Grant), who, it is ru-
mored, may have been the mistress of Quill. Her behavior
on the night in question reportedly triggered Quill's assault
on Laura Manion. As Maida and Parnell discover when they
interview local residents, Quill was well-liked by almost
everyone, whereas Laura has a notorious reputation for being an immoral flirt.

   In addition, Paul and Parnell at first find themselves
unable to uncover a legal peg on which to base their defense of Manion. However, after spending many tiring hours
in the courthouse library, they find a long-forgotten decision
in which a plea of "irresistible impulse" won a case, thereby
establishing a precedent. The fact that Manion may not
have been conscious of his actions on the night in question
remains questionable, though, for Manion did not put forward the defense of temporary insanity until Biegler prod-
ded him to come up with a legal excuse for his behavior.
But, having obtained the backing they need, Paul and Parnell need only convince the jury that Laura Manion was indeed
raped. With this in mind, they prepare for the upcoming
trial.

   Biegler is somewhat concerned with the fact that a
new judge from the lower region of Michigan has been called
to take the place of old reliable Judge Maitland, who is re-
covering from a severe illness. Biegler had decided against
waiting for Maitland's return because it would have meant having
his client sit in jail for another two or three months. However, Biegler is immediately put at ease once Judge Weaver
(Joseph N. Welch) makes his wry opening address:

> There's no need, I think, to dwell at length upon
> my methods; one judge is quite like another. The
> only difference is maybe in the state of their diges-
> tions or in their proclivities for sleeping on the
> bench. For myself, I can digest pig iron. And
> while I may appear to doze occasionally, you'll find

[Opposite:] James Stewart shouts at Brooks West as George
C. Scott looks on.

I'm easily awakened, particularly if shaken gently
by a good lawyer with a fine point of law.

No sooner are Biegler and his clients assured that
they're in safe hands, though, than they discover that Mitch
Lodwick, the prosecuting attorney, has called in as an assistant the well-known D.A. from Lansing, Claude Dancer
(George C. Scott). Dancer is smooth-talking, slick, and
arrogant and does not yield easily to defeat. He provides
the perfect contrast to Biegler's easygoing, backwoods demeanor (though Biegler can be just as cagey when he has
to; the difference is that he does not flaunt his intelligence,
as his opponent does).

At first, Lodwick and Dancer continually object to
Paul's efforts to bring up Laura Manion's rape story. Since,
as Lodwick points out, "the burden of the defense is to
prove temporary insanity at the time of the shooting and
nothing more," Judge Weaver sustains his objections. Biegler becomes increasingly convinced that the testimonies of a
physician, Dr. Raschid (Ned Weaver)--who was asked to
examine only the body of Quill--and a photographer, Mr.
Burke (Joseph Kearns)--who has brought to court pictures
of the deceased only--have been deliberately slanted by the
prosecution in order to elicit sympathy for their side. (There
is an amusing moment when Biegler asks the photographer
what happened to the pictures he took of Laura--"Didn't
they turn out?"--to which Burke, offended, snaps, "All my
pictures turn out!" which gets a hearty chuckle from the
spectators.)

Biegler's attitude toward the prosecution is not relieved by the testimony of Alphonse Paquette, who proves
himself just as hostile toward Biegler in court as he had out.
Biegler has sone fun trying to get a damaging confession
out of him, though:

> Biegler (referring to Barney Quill's passions):
> What would you call a man with an insatiable
> penchant for women?
>
> Paquette: A what?
>
> Biegler: A penchant, a desire, a longing.
>
> Paquette: A ladies' man, I guess--or maybe just a
> damn fool.

(laughter from audience)

Judge: You will confine yourself to answering the questions--the attorneys will provide the wise-cracks.

Biegler (amused by judge's quip): Can you think of another name?

Paquette (knows what he wants, but won't give it to him): Masher?

Biegler: Oh, come on, Mr. Paquette. Mashers went out with whale-bone corsets and hairnets. Did you ever hear the expression "wolf"?

Paquette: Guess so. Must have slipped my mind.

Biegler: Well, that's understandable, clanking around up there with all those rusty old mashers.... Was Barney Quill a wolf, Mr. Paquette?

Conference at the bench about Laura's panties. From left: Welch, Stewart, West, and Scott.

    Paquette: I couldn't say.

    Biegler: Or wouldn't?

    Lodwick: Objection!

    Judge: Sustained. He said he couldn't say.

When Biegler asks Paquette whether Barney Quill came
back to the bar late on the night of the shooting after raping Laura and told him to look out for Lieutenant Manion,
there is a long pause before Paquette emphatically states,
"He did not." This may indicate that he is lying, but the
audience is never positively certain.

Finally, realizing that his case may be seriously hurt-
ing, Biegler lashes out at Dancer and Lodwick, slamming his
fist down on a table: "This is a cross-examination of a murder trial, not a high-school debate! What are you and
Dancer trying to do, railroad this soldier into the clink?!"
Judge Weaver threatens to hold Biegler in contempt of court
the next time he makes such an undisciplined outburst.
Biegler apologizes to the court for his conduct and continues
his cross-examination of Mr. Lemon (Russ Brown), the operator of the trailer park where the Manions were staying on the
night of the shooting. Because he seems a decent, honest,
straightforward sort--with no obvious reasons for concealing
the truth--there is no reason to doubt the validity of his
statement that Lt. Manion came to him late on the night in
question and declared, "I think I just killed Barney Quill."
However, we are not as confident of his ability to judge
whether Manion was in complete possession of his faculties
at that moment; after all, the witness is not a psychiatrist.

The turning point in the proceedings comes when
Biegler calls Sgt. Durgo (Ken Lynch) of the local police
force to the stand. He testifies that after the shooting Lt.
Manion came to him and told him of some "trouble" he'd had
with Quill. (Biegler discovers that those were not the real
words Manion had used but were instead suggested by the
prosecution in order to make it seem to the jury as though
Manion's behavior was cool and deliberate.) However, just
when Sgt. Durgo is about to divulge what Lt. Manion actually said to him (that Barney Quill had raped his wife),
Lodwick raises an objection: "The burden of the defense
is to prove temporary insanity at the time of the shooting.

Paul begs the court, "Let me cut into the apple."   (Photo
courtesy of UCLA film stills archive)

Instead, what the defense is trying to do is introduce some
sensational material with the purpose of obscuring the real
issues." Biegler counters by asking, "Your Honor, how can
the jury accurately estimate the testimony given at this trial
unless they first know the reason behind it: why Lt. Manion shot Barney Quill. Now, the prosecution would like to
separate the motive from the act. Well, that's like trying to
take the core from an apple without breaking the skin. Now,
the core of our defense is that the defendant's temporary insanity was somehow triggered by this so-called 'trouble' with
Quill. And I beg the court--I beg the court--to let me cut
into the apple."

After a short pause, the judge rules in Biegler's favor,
thereby paving the way for a discussion of Laura's rape.
However, the judge calls all three attorneys to the bench
when Durgo brings up the fact that he and his men searched
in vain for "a certain undergarment" of Mrs. Manion's. The
resulting conference is one of the comic highlights of courtroom drama history:

> Judge: What exactly was the name of the under-
> garment?
>
> Biegler: Panties, Your Honor.
>
> Judge: There's a certain light connotation attached
> to the word "panties." Can we find another
> name for them?
>
> Lodwick: I never heard my wife call them anything
> else.
>
> Judge: Mr. Biegler?
>
> Biegler: I'm a bachelor, Your Honor.
>
> Judge: That's a great help. Mr. Dancer?
>
> Dancer: I was overseas during the war, Your
> Honor. I learned a French word. I'm afraid
> it might be slightly suggestive.
>
> Judge: Most French words are. All right, be
> seated, gentlemen.

As with most of the judge's remarks throughout the film,
the following seems to be addressed to a wider audience
than just the spectators in the courtroom:

Dancer coaxes damaging evidence from Laura. (Photo
courtesy of UCLA film stills archive)

For the benefit of the jury, but more especially
for the spectators, the undergarment referred to in
the testimony was, to be exact, Mrs. Manion's panties ... [pause while he waits for a snicker in the
courtroom to subside]. I wanted you to get your
snickering over and done with. This pair of panties will be mentioned again in the course of this
trial and when that happens there will not be one
laugh, one snicker, one giggle or even one smirk
in my courtroom. There isn't anything comic about
a pair of panties that figure in the violent death of
one man and in the possible incarceration of another.

Again, as was the case with Mr. Lemon, the credibility of
Sgt. Durgo's testimony is limited by the boundaries of his
own intellect. Though he is undoubtedly sincere when he
says that Mrs. Manion had "big black bruises over her face
and arms," he is really not qualified to judge Lt. Manion's
mental state at the time of the shooting.

The real tension of the courtroom sequence unfolds
when Dancer cross-examines Laura Manion. Dancer hints
that what really happened on the night in question was that
Laura, who had been having an affair with Quill for some
time, was beaten by her husband when he caught her com-
ing home late with Quill. Dancer's contention that Manion
is an insanely jealous husband who will not hesitate to use
violence to protect (or reprimand) his wife whenever necessary is supported by several eyewitness accounts from
friends of the couple. Furthermore, a doctor (Howard
McNear) who examined Laura testifies that no physical evidence of sperm was found in her body. However, he admits that this is not conclusive proof that she was not
raped: "It's impossible to tell whether a mature, married
woman has been raped," he declares--though what her being "mature" (a mental term) or "married" (a legal term)
has to do with her condition is unclear; again, the imperfections of human perception are exposed. Also, under
Dancer's rapid-fire interrogation, Laura makes a damaging
admission: that Manion made her swear on a rosary that
she had indeed been raped by Quill. Dancer skillfully leads
her to admit that since she consciously decided to get a
divorce from her first husband--thereby ignoring one of the
cardinal rules of the Catholic Church, of which she was a
member--the validity of her oath on a sacred emblem could

Laura's dog takes a liking to Dancer.   (Photo courtesy of
UCLA film stills archive)

easily be questioned. When he asks her a second time why
she chose to swear on the rosary--"Would your husband
think you'd lie about a thing like being raped by Quill?"--
she manages only a lame response: "Because I wasn't making much sense." In addition, when he blatantly asks her
whether she is Barney Quill's mistress and whether that was
the first time she'd been in his car late at night, she pauses
for a long time before denying both charges (possibly out of
fear of being caught lying under oath, as Paquette had done
earlier). During this scene, Preminger continually cuts to
reaction shots of Lt. Manion. His wife's final denial apparently relieves his suspicions (he had been cold and indifferent to her throughout the trial)--perhaps Dancer was right?
--and the two of them share a moment of intimacy after she
steps off the stand.

The almost unbearable tension of these scenes is relieved when Biegler, in an attempt to give Laura confidence
on the stand, offers to show the court how remarkably intelligent her little terrier Muff is (the dog had carried a
flashlight in its mouth on the night of the murder). Sur-
prisingly, once the animal is let loose it runs straight to
Dancer and jumps in his lap, providing everyone with a few
moments of amusement. Biegler quips, "Muff sure doesn't
know who his enemies are."

While all this has been going on, Parnell has been doing a bit of private detective work in the region of Canada
just north of the Upper Peninsula. In the process he has
almost succeeded in killing himself (he borrowed Maida's car,
but hasn't driven in twenty years). When Biegler visits
him in the hospital, he is informed by Parnell that Mary
Pilant, the girl suspected of having been Barney Quill's
mistress, is in actuality Quill's illegitimate daughter.

With this knowledge, Biegler confronts Mary, explain-
ing to her his contention that Alphonse Paquette is withhold-
ing knowledge that Barney Quill told him he had in fact
raped Laura for the sake of protecting Mary's image of her
father as a kind, loving man. Biegler tells her that "in my
business I've had to learn that people aren't just all good or
all bad but people are many things" and also that "everybody
loves something, or someone. Me, I love fishing, and an old
guy by the name of Parnell. Manion loves his freedom--he'd
like a little more of it. Barney loved you. And so does Al."

Biegler's speech gives the message of the film in a nutshell:
the fact that, when one is dealing with human beings, the
question of personal motives often becomes so involved that
it is almost impossible to distinguish truth from fiction; indeed, the viewer will never know whether Biegler's hunch
about Al was correct, for Al, despite Biegler's request that
he return to court, never does so.

Back in court, Lt. Manion, having been called to the
stand, tells Biegler that the shots he fired on the night in
question "don't seem to be connected with me ... they seem
distant, far away." Here is almost conclusive evidence of
Manion's scheming: when Manion first told Biegler of his actions back in the jail at the beginning of the film, he made
no indication that he hadn't been conscious of his actions at
the time; his testimony now is undoubtedly the result of his
subsequent knowledge of the conditions under which dissocia-
tive reaction, or "irresistible impulse," occurs. An Army
psychiatrist, Dr. Smith (Orson Bean), supports the theory
that Manion, upon seeing what had happened to his wife,
was "seized by an impulse that he was powerless to control"
and forced to shoot Quill. The psychiatrist for the state,

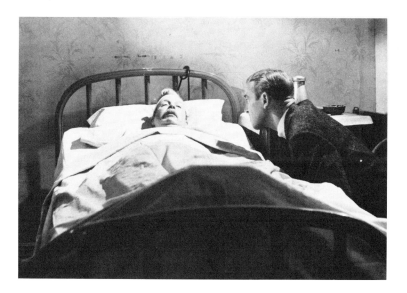

Paul visits Parnell in the hospital.

Paul tries to get Mary Pilant (Kathryn Grant) to come to court as a witness for the defense.

Dr. Harcourt (Alexander Campbell), disagrees, claiming that Manion was completely conscious of his actions at the time. His testimony, however, is not based upon an examination of the defendant, as Dr. Smith's is.

Fearing that the defense may be gaining ground, the prosecution calls in a last-minute "surprise" witness, a man named Duane Miller (Don Ross), who shared a cell with Manion at the Iron City Jail and whom Manion had harmed when Miller said something nasty about Laura. Miller claims that Manion told him he was going to make up a story that would "fool all them corncobbers on the jury" and that when he got out of jail he was going to "kick that bitch (Laura) to Kingdom Come." Manion, hysterical, shouts "Liar! You're a lousy stinkin' liar!" forcing Biegler to come to his aid.

Paul submits panties as exhibit #1 for the defense. (Photo courtesy of UCLA film stills archive)

"My client's outburst is almost excusable, Your Honor, since the prosecution has seen fit to put a felon on the stand to testify against an officer of the United States Army," he declares. Obviously James Stewart put a lot of his own deep respect for the American military into his indictment of Miller; the word "felon" registers as unpleasantly on his face as if he'd just swallowed a rotten egg. Biegler discredits Miller by reading his lengthy criminal record to the jury and by hinting that the prosecution (who had talked with Miller privately before his appearance) had promised the witness a lighter sentence if he sided with them. "I don't feel I can dignify this creature with any more questions," Biegler declares. Preminger and Mayes nicely contrast the bearing of the "humble country lawyer"--as Biegler calls himself--and that of the "brilliant prosecutor from the big city of Lansing,"

as he labels Dancer with sarcastic humility, by having Biegler refuse a private conference with his client in spite of
the shocking testimony of Miller (Dancer had requested numerous unnecessary conferences--mainly for show purposes--
throughout the trial).

Finally, to Biegler's surprise, Mary Pilant shows up
in court. She has brought Laura Manion's ripped panties,
which she had found the morning after the murder in the
laundry chute of the hotel in which she and Barney Quill
lived. Holding them up, Biegler emphasizes the fact that
they are "badly torn, as if they'd been ripped apart by
powerful hands." Dancer attacks her testimony by suggesting that she can't know for sure that Quill dropped
them in the chute (which is true) and that she brought them
to court in a hasty attempt at revenge for Quill's leaving
her for Laura Manion. However, Dancer's entire plan of
action is embarrassingly discredited by her statement that
she was not Quill's mistress but rather his daughter.

The next morning, the jury finds Manion "not guilty
by reason of insanity." However, when Paul and Parnell
head out to the Manions' trailer park with a promissory note
for the lieutenant to sign, they find a hastily scribbled note
reading, "Dear Mr. Biegler, Sorry but I had to leave town
suddenly--I was seized by an irresistible impulse.--Frederick
Manion." "Now that's what I call poetic justice for everybody," Parnell remarks of this final ironic twist, indicating
that Biegler got out of the case not what he (or, more accurately, Maida) had hoped for (the fee)--as retribution for
his cynical manipulations throughout the course of the trial--
but instead, because of the persistent respect for the law
which he demonstrated throughout the case, he has acquired
a new, alcohol-free law partner (Parnell) and a new client
(Mary Pilant, who has entrusted them with managing her late
father's estate). Manion's evasion of the debt throws doubt
upon the accuracy of the jury's verdict and leaves one won-
dering whether justice was done to him after all.

The verdict itself is left in doubt, too--the jury make
no mention of "irresistible impulse," the core of Biegler's
whole defense--and we are shown how the jury are being
confused. In fact, as Parnell had remarked just before the
verdict was given, it is a miracle that "twelve people of vary-
ing shapes and sizes who are called into a room to judge

another human being as different from them as they are from
each other" are able to reach a decision at all. But, because they always manage somehow, "God bless juries," he
remarks. We have already seen just how difficult the process of obtaining unanimity in a jury is in 12 Angry Men.
By making the outcome of the trial a dubious one, Preminger
has forced those of the viewing audience to become the jury
and decide for themselves what really happened to the Manions on the night in question. Preminger's point is that the
law cannot guarantee justice. All it can do is to try to ensure that every step toward a verdict be taken fairly and
justly. Since, as mentioned earlier, this is a character study
and not a murder mystery (as was the earlier Witness for
the Prosecution), the audience is not terribly concerned
with the ultimate verdict of the jury. Indeed, this was
Preminger's intention: a shot of the foreman giving the
verdict quickly dissolves to a shot of Paul and Parnell driv-
ing to the trailer park. One could even go so far as to say
that since so many issues have already been left unresolved

Welch and Traver, who became the best of friends. (Photo
courtesy of UCLA film stills archive)

by this time--for instance, the fact that we never found out
whether it was a rape or seduction which triggered Manion's
shooting of Quill--that the verdict itself comes as a sort of
anticlimax to the preceding action; in fact, it is almost meaningless, except that it shows how the jury are being confused.

The Laura Manion character is the pivot around which
everything else hinges; it was her tale of rape that started
everything. According to Wendell Mayes, the abundance of
ambiguity was deliberate on the part of himself and Preminger: "I tried very hard to counter every apparent truth
with a strong doubt. The only things one might begin to
realize were truths were that Mrs. Manion was a victim one
way or another and that Manion did in fact murder Quill,
whether consciously or otherwise."[13] It is precisely this
unrelenting emphasis on the ambiguity of human motives
that places Anatomy above all other courtroom films--and
which makes watching it again and again a new and reward-
ing experience each time.

In addition to the film's primary concerns with the
social aspect of a trial and the reliability of the jury system,
there are scattered about a number of other smaller--but
equally relevant--comments about the nature of the judicial
system. For instance, there is the preoccupation of the defense and prosecution with "impressing" the jury (primarily
through nonintellectual means; the basic assumption is that
juries are composed of people who are not very bright).
When Dr. Smith greets Parnell at the train station, the latter is disappointed that Smith is not a German ("A name like
Ludwig Von Smith would sit better with a jury," he remarks)
and not an older (and hence more experienced-looking) gentleman. There is also Paul Biegler's comment to Lt. Manion
that it is not humanly possible for a jury to disregard what
it has already heard, despite the fact that the letter of the
law would often require them to do so. In addition, because
the situations in the trial scenes are arranged realistically,
the audience is made to understand that not every shred of
testimony is pertinent to the final outcome of the trial; indeed, as stated earlier, the verdict becomes of very little
concern to those watching the proceedings, for this film is
an examination (an anatomy of a trial, as the title suggests),
a puzzle in which all the pieces do not necessarily fit together in harmony.

Despite the fact that, in adapting the Traver novel
for the screen, Wendell Mayes eliminated the highly detailed
closing summations of both prosecution and defense and also
Judge Weaver's charging of the jury (due to the fact that
the script was getting too long, he told me), his screenplay
does a remarkable job of illuminating the little ambiguities of
character and of capturing much of Traver's concern with
the imperfections of the legal system.   Its most exceptional
feature is that it manages to tackle such unpleasant subjects
as rape and murder with unabashed candor while at the same
time remaining always highly entertaining--many of the hu-
morous lines (most of which have to do with Laura's sexiness
in one way or another) have been noted throughout.   The
use of certain clinical vocabulary words--such as "contra-
ceptive," "sexual climax," and "spermatogenesis"--to describe the rape became a source of much controversy, however, as they had never before been heard onscreen.   In
fact, the film almost never got shown in Chicago, where a
Catholic censorship board was determined to see to it that

Dancer bears down on Mary Pilant.   (Photo courtesy of
UCLA film stills archive)

all the "objectionable" phrases were eliminated before the
public would be allowed to see the film. However, Preminger characteristically refused to comply, and the judge trying the case found in his favor. "It was a famous victory,"
Willi Frischauer recalls.[14] It is obvious, if one looks at
Preminger's earlier efforts, that he selected the Traver
novel largely because of its sensational subject matter. However, as Time's reviewer noted, his film of Anatomy "dis-
plays an attitude toward sex that is more wholesome than
the merely sniggering spirit that prevails in many a movie."[15]
And, as the New York Herald Tribune's critic stated, "They
don't use the words because they want to but because they
have to."[16] By today's standards such material seems tame
indeed, but its relevance to the story is still obvious.

Anatomy of a Murder features many of the "classic"
elements of courtroom drama evidenced in countless previous
efforts, both major and minor: the humble country lawyer
versus the city slicker, with the former defeating the latter
by virtue of his essential honesty; the drunken sidekick who
risks his life for one last chance at fighting for justice; the
witty, unpaid secretary of the hero; the last-minute "surprise" witness. Yet, despite the fact that these characters
and situations may seem at first glance like cliches, their
presence in Anatomy is so enlivened by Wendell Mayes' wonderfully contemporary dialogue that they seem almost new
creations entirely.

Preminger's direction is meticulous, his camera rest-
less and constantly highlighting nuances of character and
the ambiguous nature of certain situations (often during the
trial sequence witnesses are photographed at slightly slanted
angles, in order to make them seem suspicious) and thereby
increasing suspense as the trial wages on. The most strik-
ing example of Preminger's directorial flair overcoming what
could have proven to be a shortcoming in the script occurs
when Dancer interrogates Mary Pilant at the conclusion of
the trial. We, the audience, already know (from Parnell's
earlier revelation to Paul) that Mary is Barney Quill's daughter, not his mistress, and that the minute she reveals this
fact to Dancer his entire line of questioning will be hopelessly dismissed. However, we remain riveted to our seats precisely because Preminger has wisely decided to opt for suspense rather than surprise; he concentrates so closely on
Dancer's menacing features and Mary's wide-eyed, terrified

"Dear Mr. Biegler: had to leave suddenly. Was seized by an 'irresistible impulse.'" (Photo courtesy of UCLA film stills archive)

countenance that the viewer simply does not have time to think about the logic behind the sequence.

Achieving this was no small accomplishment, considering that the trial was shot in a real courtroom, where the natural boundaries posed a formidable challenge to the crew. "You can't move walls," Preminger remarked.[17] Preminger uses long shots mainly, a practice with which he had recently become very familiar--his last film, Porgy and Bess (1959) had been shot in the TODD-AO process, making long takes mandatory--and close-ups sparingly, so that when they do appear they are used to full advantage (as when Claude Dancer closes in on Mary Pilant). The trial sequence, which comprises almost two thirds of the film's nearly three-hour running time, is, to be expected, the highlight of the picture, and most of the credit for its success goes to Preminger. He builds the battle between defense and prosecution ever so smoothly, allowing for small triumphs on both sides while subtly building tension and exposing the traits that make the characters stand out (for example, Paul Biegler's habit of making fish hooks to help him think; this recalls Sir Wilfrid Robarts' arranging his blood-pressure pills in Witness for the Prosecution). We are given roughly a full hour to get to know the major personalities in the story before the trial begins. It lasts, almost without a break, for the remaining hour and forty minutes. By the time it has ended and we reach the memorable scene in Paul's study in which he, Parnell, and Maida wearily await the call from the courthouse to return for the verdict, we are just as worn out as they, due to Preminger's success in involving us so closely in the proceedings. To an outsider the film may appear lengthy, but there is hardly a dull moment throughout, thanks to the combined efforts of Preminger and Mayes, assisted in no small measure by Sam Leavitt's authentically drab, cold-looking photography, perfect in keeping with the general tone of the film and in capturing the atmosphere of the Ishpeming and Marquette communities and contrasting the homeless Manions with the lifelong residents of the towns; by editor Lou Loeffler, who enlivens the courtroom sequences immeasurably by providing constant visual variety; by Saul Bass' inventive credit-title sequence, in which the hands of a dismembered body reach out helplessly and blacken the screen when Preminger's name appears, indicating that it's up to him to "solve the puzzle," as it were; and lastly by the score of Duke Ellington.

Ellington's contribution to Anatomy is unique: he was called by Preminger to come to Michigan with the rest of the cast so that he could develop his score gradually as the picture was shot, a practice uncommon in Hollywood.   Usually the producer or director hires the composer after shooting is completed.   Preminger chose Ellington primarily for two reasons: first, he "wanted an authentic jazz score.   In the film, Paul Biegler is a jazz fan, and thus this kind of music, more than any other, would reflect the tastes of the hero. Moreover, Preminger was of the opinion that a jazz score would be the ideal counterpart for a story of the intricate legal proceedings of a murder trial.   Still another factor ... was that Ellington had never composed a film score.   Preminger felt that this very newness could produce a freshness which an experienced composer might no longer possess."[18]

The final score provides just the right surface brittleness and underlying hints of urgency for commenting upon the motives of the principal characters, Laura Manion in particular.   Unfortunately, however, the score is often abruptly broken up during the first hour and then not employed at all during the trial sequences; listeners who would like to hear it in its full form should purchase the soundtrack album from the film--which, by the way, has recently been reissued.   Incidentally, Preminger was so pleased with Ellington's work that he gave him a cameo role in the film as a piano player named "Pie-Eye" at a roadside cafe.   He performs his own "Happy Anatomy" piece with James Stewart in that scene.

Perhaps the most admirable aspect of Preminger's direction is its self-effacement in favor of his actors--so much so that, in nominating the film for seven Academy Awards, the MPAAS neglected to include one for Best Director.   Heading the cast is James Stewart, who gives one of his most complete and authoritative characterizations as Biegler.   Along with his performances in Frank Capra's Mr. Smith Goes to Washington (1939) and It's a Wonderful Life (1946), this one marks a summit in his long and distinguished career.   Because the entire film is seen through his eyes, he is present more than 95 percent of the time, making this his longest screen appearance to date.   Preminger's choice of Stewart for the role of Biegler (a.k.a. John Voelker, who actually bears a closer physical resemblance to John Wayne) was a brilliant stroke: the role gave Stewart the chance to combine

both the homespun, boyish qualities of his 1930s and 1940s
work with the cagey, razor-sharp sensibility of his Anthony
Mann and Alfred Hitchcock heroes. The result is possibly
the most true-to-life Stewart characterization. He was given
the Best Actor Award at the Venice Film Festival and the
New York Critics Award for Best Actor for his performance.
Likewise, Lee Remick, as the sexpot wife, and Ben Gazzara,
as the jealous lieutenant, are also commendable. They succeed in making their characters necessarily equivocal but
always believable. Actually, Lana Turner was Preminger's
first choice for the role of Laura, but she resigned after a
dispute about the type of clothing the wife of a penniless
Army lieutenant should wear. This was fortunate, for the
role of Laura is one that requires brains as well as sexiness,
both of which Lee Remick possesses in great quantities.
Arthur O'Connell's downtrodden appearance convinced Preminger in an interview that he was Parnell, and he is ever so
delightful as the sozzled but enthusiastic attorney. George
C. Scott gives a brilliant, multifaceted performance as Claude
Dancer. This was his first notable screen role. The entire
supporting cast, down to the smallest bit part, is commendable also: Eve Arden as Stewart's witty secretary; Kathryn
Grant as the timid Mary Pilant; Murray Hamilton as the abrasive Alphonse Paquette; and Brooks West as Dancer's overly
ambitious courtroom ally. Seldom has a cast of this size
responded so enthusiastically to direction--and this is surprising, considering the strenuous conditions which plagued
their shooting in the frozen Upper Peninsula.

    The performance about which the critics at the time
raved most, however, was that of Joseph N. Welch. Though
not an actor, Welch managed to inject so much natural charm
and spunk into his role as the judge that he more than justified Preminger's hunch that a real judge would be the ideal
choice for the role. Welch and Traver, incidentally, became
the best of friends, and were even planning on collaborating
on a book, when Welch died in late 1960 at age 69.

    Anatomy proved to be the biggest critical and commer-
cial success of Preminger's career. Traver attributes this to
the fact that "contrary to the usual Otto-the-autocrat leg-
ends, he not only consulted both Joseph N. Welch and me on
the filming, but listened closely to what we said."[19] Perhaps the reason that Anatomy is so much more satisfying a
work than any of Preminger's other films as producer-director

is that he exhibited a firmer control over his material on this occasion (he also managed to avoid getting into fights with his players this time around; future squabbles with actors would prove detrimental to efforts like Exodus (1960; Paul Newman and Lee J. Cobb) and The Cardinal (1963; Tom Tryon).

Preminger's preference for long takes and sustained objective point of view proved to be best suited to black-and-white features which, like Anatomy, involved an investigation of some sort. Hence, Advise and Consent (1962) and Bunny Lake Is Missing (1965) are fascinating anatomies of corruption in political circles and of the disappearance of a small child, respectively, and Exodus (1960) is an expected let-down. No one (especially not Leon Uris, author of the original novel, who sued Preminger for damaging his original conception) could have expected the passion suggested by the subject and by Ernest Gold's Oscar-winning theme to emerge for a second with the Preminger objectivity ever-present.

There is no denying, however, that Anatomy remains the quintessential Preminger film in terms of its clean, classical style and its probing analysis of a vital aspect of society, the law. It was also an important film in terms of cinema history, for it showed that, "at a time when a film's average running time was still around 90 minutes ... a nearly three-hour-long picture did not have to be a road-show color spectacular in order to succeed at the box-office, and could be as tightly structured and consistently engrossing as the best of conventional-length dramas."[20]

Preminger's dedication to his craft was put to the test seven years after Anatomy's release, in 1966, when he took Columbia and Screen Gems, a subsidiary, to court because Columbia had sold Anatomy as part of a package of sixty films to ABC-TV in New York, where its 160-minute run was interrupted thirteen times with a total of thirty-six commercials. "The commercial interruptions destroy the value of the picture!" Preminger declared.[21] According to Willi Frischauser, "a big principle was at stake: the right of a director to protect the artistic integrity of his work." Elia Kazan, the director of such acclaimed dramas as On the Waterfront (1954) and East of Eden (1955), showed up in defense of Preminger. Preminger unfortunately lost his case, but his arguments were well-publicized.

Today, twenty-five years and several courtroom films later, Anatomy of a Murder still stands as the best of the Hollywood rest. Its frankness of presentation, its painstaking devotion to realism in approach and setting, and its strict adherence to actual legal procedure while being itself something of an indictment of the legal system place it far above the traditional melodramatic Hollywood courtroomer.

NOTES

1. Robert Traver, Introduction to Anatomy of a Murder, 25th anniversary edition (New York: St. Martin's Press, 1983).

2. Richard Griffith, Anatomy of a Motion Picture (New York: St. Martin's Press, 1959), p. 7.

3. Griffith, p. 8.

4. Griffith, p. 11.

5. Griffith, p. 13.

6. Griffith, p. 14.

7. Otto Preminger, Preminger: An Autobiography (Garden City, New York: Doubleday & Co., 1977), p. 154.

8. Willi Frischauer, Behind the Scenes of Otto Preminger: An Unauthorized Biography (New York: William Morrow & Co., 1974), pp. 171-72.

9. Griffith, pp. 25-26, 28.

10. Robert Traver, preface to Griffith, p. 3.

11. Adam Garbicz and Jacek Klinowski, Cinema, The Magic Vehicle: A Guide to its Achievement, vol. 2 (New York: Schocken Books, 1983), p. 466.

12. Wendell Mayes, Unpublished Screenplay for Anatomy of a Murder (Carlyle Productions Inc., 1959). All future references to dialogue come from here.

13. Letter from Mayes to author, dated July 2, 1985.

14. Frischauer, p. 176.

15. Time, June 13, 1959, p. 68.

16. Paul V. Beckley, review of Anatomy in New York Herald Tribune, July 3, 1959.

17. Frischauer, p. 174.

18. Griffith, p. 105.

19. Traver, Introduction to Anatomy of a Murder.

20. Jean-Pierre Coursodon and Pierre Sauvage, article on Otto Preminger in American Directors, vol. 1 (New York: McGraw-Hill, 1983), p. 270.

21. Frischauer, p. 178.

Chapter 6

INHERIT THE WIND

Credits

A Lomitas Production, released through United Artists, 1960. Producer and Director: Stanley Kramer. Screenplay: Nathan E. Douglas and Harold Jacob Smith, based on the play by Jerome Lawrence and Robert E. Lee. Director of Photography: Ernest Laszlo, A.S.C. Editor: Frederic Knudtson, A.C.E. Music: Ernest Gold. Production Designer: Rudolph Sternad. Production Manager: Clem Beauchamp. Assistant Director: Ivan Volkman. Assistant to the Producer: Anne P. Kramer. Technical Advisor: Rev. Thomas R. Marshall. Sound Engineer: Joe Lapis. Camera Operator: Charles Wheeler. Sound Editor: Walter Elliott, M.P.S.E. Wardrobe: Joe King. Company Grip: Morris Rosen. Assistant Company Grip: Martin Kashuk. Script Supervisor: Sam Freedle. Vocals: Leslie Uggams. Makeup: Bud Westmore. Property Master: Art Cole. Chief Gaffer: Roy Roberts. Hair Stylist: Larry Germain. Casting: Stalmaster-Lister. Black-and-white. Running time: 127 minutes.

Cast: Spencer Tracy (Henry Drummond), Fredric March (Matthew Harrison Brady), Gene Kelly (E.K. Hornbeck), Dick York (Bertram Cates), Donna Anderson (Rachel Brown), Florence Eldridge (Mrs. Brady), Harry Morgan (Judge), Elliott Reid (Davenport), Philip Coolidge (Major), Claude Akins (Reverend Brown), Paul Hartman (Meeker), Jimmy Boyd (Howard), Noah Beery, Jr. (Stebbins), Gordon Polk

(Sillers), Ray Teal (Dunlap), Norman Fell (Radio Announcer), Hope Summers (Mrs. Krebs), Renee Godfrey (Mrs.
Stebbins).

Another prominent figure in the realms of independent
producers in addition to Otto Preminger was Stanley Kramer.
Unlike Preminger, who had begun his career as a director
and had later taken on the added task of producing his pictures, Kramer started out as and became indelibly associated
with the term "producer." Kramer was the first individual
to challenge the sacred taboos of the Hollywood Production
Code by making films about such unpopular issues as corruption in the boxing field (Champion [1949], directed by Mark
Robson and starring Kirk Douglas) and antiblack prejudice
(Robson's Home of the Brave [1949]). Although director
Elia Kazan had tackled similar issues in his Gentleman's
Agreement (1947), in which Gregory Peck posed as a Jew to
investigate anti-Semitism in the business world, and in Pinky
(1949), with Jeanne Crain as a light-skinned Negro passing
for white, the Kramer productions remain the most durable
today due to their uncompromising sincerity and forcefulness
of tone.

It was after Kramer took on the additional task of di-
recting his pictures with Not as a Stranger (1955), a tribute
to the workings of the medical profession, that he began to
be labeled (unfavorably) as the representative of the so-
called "liberal school of message movies." These "message
movies" were films with a conscious intent to teach lessons,
locate dangers, and correct unworthy attitudes.[1] The Defi-
ant Ones (1958), another pioneering (like Home of the Brave)
and memorable racial drama with Sidney Poitier and Tony
Curtis, concerned the plight of two bitterly opposed ex-
convicts, one black and one white, who escape from a chain
gang but remain handcuffed to each other. It holds up well
today as a quietly powerful study of the endurance of the
human spirit. On the Beach (1959) was a solid, serious,
and bleak but ponderous look at the aftermath of a nuclear
explosion and its effects on the members of an Australian
community. It pales in intensity and interest next to Sidney
Lumet's Fail-Safe (1964). Kramer has admitted more than
once that his earnestness to get his points across at any
cost has on occasion resulted in heavy-handed treatment of
potentially interesting subjects. Nevertheless, one cannot
fault him for his effort.

Kramer's next film after On the Beach, Inherit the
Wind (1960), was an adaptation of the Jerome Lawrence/
Robert E. Lee Broadway smash dramatizing the famed 1925
"Monkey Trial" held in Dayton, Tennessee, during which
Clarence Darrow defended John T. Scopes, a high school
biology teacher who propounded (in violation of state law)
Darwin's theory of evolution to his pupils. William Jennings
Bryan was the prosecuting attorney. Prior to the release
of the film, Kramer issued an extended personal statement
which included his reasons for taking on the new project:

> For me, Inherit the Wind completes a trilogy of
> what have been called by some "controversial" pic-
> tures of which the first two were The Defiant Ones
> and On the Beach. Enjoy them or not--agree with
> them or not--these are motion pictures that hit peo-
> ple hard, force people to see them, to think and to
> take a stand.... From the standpoint of box-office,
> I think people want thought-provoking material on
> the movie screen--something they can't get on their
> home screen. The success of The Defiant Ones and
> other films of that nature would seem to back that
> up. [2]

The seriousness behind Kramer's intentions is at once
evident from the atmosphere surrounding the credit titles:
an undercurrent of solemn urgency characterizes Ernest
Gold's theme as a group of determined, stony-faced town officials of Hillsboro, Tennessee, gather one by one near the
Hillsboro courthouse and march toward the local high school.
Bertram Cates (prototype of John T. Scopes; Dick York),
the biology teacher, is arrested while attempting to explain
Darwin's theory of evolution to his students, a violation of
a state law forbidding the teaching of any scientific principles or theories believed inconsistent with the Bible.

As Cates sits alone in his jail cell, the news is spread
that Matthew Harrison Brady (prototype of William Jennings
Bryan), the three-time Presidential candidate and avowed
Fundamentalist, has been appointed prosecutor of the case.
The hellfire-and-brimstone philosophy of the Hillsboro community is put at ease, but only long enough to let their real
interests become apparent: one member of a town meeting
smiles greedily as he contemplates the amount of business
Brady's presence will drum up for the area: "All those

Brady (Fredric March), Mrs. Brady (Florence Eldridge), and
Reverend Brown (Claude Akins) at a rally for Brady.

folks are gonna need someplace to eat." Already the scenarists have established the ridiculousness of these pea-
brained yokels and their specious religious ideals. They are
not unlike the townsfolk of Pickett, Arkansas, whom Budd
Schulberg and Elia Kazan ridiculed in their satire on the
gullibility of the American TV-watching public, A Face in
the Crowd (1957).

Cates and his fiancée, Rachel Brown (Donna Anderson),
are soon introduced to cynical reporter E.K. Hornbeck (prototype of H.L. Mencken, who covered the Scopes trial; Gene
Kelly) of the Baltimore Herald, who appears to have a handy
reservation (conveyed in clever turns of phrase) about the
character of everyone involved in the proceedings but who
assures Cates that he's rooting for him ("I may be rancid
butter, but I'm on your side of the bread"). His paper has

"I had a nice clean place to stay, madam, and I left it to come here," says Gene Kelly. Spencer Tracy looks on.

hired the renowned agnostic and brilliant attorney Henry Drummond (prototype of Clarence Darrow) to defend Cates.

News of Drummond's imminent arrival arouses the towns-people's indignation, prominently displayed on picket signs ("Keep Satan out of Hillsboro," "Godliness, not gorillas," "Don't pin a tail on me") with which Bryan (Fredric March) is triumphantly welcomed to Hillsboro. With his broad, beaming, assured smile, unmistakable orator's air, and ability to spout Bible passages verbatim off the top of his head, he quickly soothes the worried souls of his fellow God-fearing citizens. However, Hornbeck, who has been observing the procession with disgust, openly denounces Bryan and reminds everyone present that the Herald will see to it that Drummond's participation in the trial is played up to the limit. When asked by a money-hungry Hillsboro woman whether he needs a clean room for the night, he replies with polite disdain, "I <u>had</u> a nice clean place to stay, madam, and I left it to come here."

The contrast between Brady and his opponent, Drummond (Spencer Tracy), is established when the latter arrives in Hillsboro--inconspicuously, on a community bus--and refuses a ride into town from a local passerby. He needs no fanfare to reassure himself of his importance in the proceedings. When a woman hears him quote a line from the Holy Scriptures (though in a skeptical manner), she says to him with reverence, "You must be a man of God," to which he replies, "No, ulcers." He greets Brady warmly (it turns out the two are old political allies who have suddenly found themselves on opposite sides of an issue for the first time). Drummond never passes up an opportunity to convey his unfaltering conviction in his cause, especially when he can irritate his opponent by rubbing in his point, as he does by answering Brady's inquiry as to how they've suddenly drifted apart with, "Well, that's evolution for you." He reminds Brady, Hornbeck, and the students in Cates' biology class that "there are no total victories" and that he did not come to Hillsboro to denounce Fundamentalism but rather to "defend Cates' right to be different." His unabashed willingness to stand alone for what he believes is nicely contrasted with Brady's insecurity and dependence on his followers in one visual composition by director Kramer: Brady and company feast together at a large table in the courthouse commissary while Drummond sits by himself at a small table in the foreground and contents himself with a sandwich.

The start of the trial commences the inevitable conflict between the shallow (but strongly upheld) traditions of the smalltown folk who are siding with Brady and the efforts of Drummond to open their minds to new ways of thinking. Drummond tells the judge (Hary Morgan) straight off that the consistent references to his opponent's title of Colonel (in the state militia) "prejudices the case of my client: it calls up a picture of the prosecution, astride a white horse, ablaze in the uniform of a militia colonel, with all the forces of right and righteousness marshalled behind him." The mayor and judge, instead of sensing the logic in Drummond's statement and acting accordingly (by requesting that the title not be used), merely betray their blind devotion to idiotic hicktown customs by appointing Drummond a temporary

Rev. Brown begs the Lord to strike down his daughter
(Donna Anderson).

Honorary Colonel--thereby, in their view, rendering the two men of equal stature.

The feud between Drummond and Brady is kindled early on when Drummond makes a mockery of one of Brady's choices for jurymen. After Brady announces his satisfaction that the farmer on the stand is an "honest, God-fearing man" and therefore a suitable choice, Drummond, fearing that the man is too biased in favor of Brady, asks him, "How are you?" To his reply, "Kinda hot," Drummond says, "So am I. Excused."

While the trial of Bertram Cates rages on, his fiancée, Rachel, finds herself torn between her love for Cates and her respect for the teachings of her father, Reverend Brown (Claude Akins). In one startingly intense scene, reminiscent of the fiery atmosphere in Richard Brooks' Elmer Gantry, another 1960 release, the Reverend kneels before a candle in his living room and vows to Jesus that he will "tear out the stony heart of flesh" of his rebellious daughter, who

March at the witness stand with Kelly, York, and Tracy in back.

stands above him, horrified that her own father could damn
her before Christ. Later, at a late-night gathering of citizens on the courthouse lawn to hear the Reverend speak
about Cates, he openly beckons the Lord to "strike down
this sinner" (meaning Rachel). Even Matthew Harrison
Brady, a devoutly religious man, is taken aback by this
gesture and reminds the Reverend of the verse in Proverbs
11 which states: "He that troubleth his own house shall
inherit the wind." This is a nice bit of foreshadowing on
the scenarists' part, for it is exactly these words which will
be used by Drummond to explain Brady's demise at the end
of the film.

Another less unsettling episode on Brady's front porch
helps to illustrate the fact that although Brady and Drummond are bitter foes in court, they are still old friends who
have weathered the times together and survived. As the
two men relax on rocking chairs, Drummond attempts to explain the source of his skepticism regarding the theory that
a perfect being exists who controls all human actions from
the heavens above. When he was a boy, he wanted more
than anything a beautiful rocking horse named Golden Dancer which was kept in a store's display window. However,
when he was finally given the toy as a present and then
tried to ride it, it collapsed. "Golden Dancer was all shine
and no substance," he tells Brady. The experience taught
him to "look behind the paint" from that point on whenever
he saw something "bright, shining, perfect-seeming."

Despite the attitudes expressed outside of the courtroom, however, the battle wages on as strongly as ever
within those hallowed walls. Brady startles the defense
when he calls Rachel Brown to the stand (Hornbeck to
Cates: "Sit down, Samson--you're about to get a haircut"). He forces her to recall the reason for Bertram
Cates' abandoning the church. Cates had seen Rev. Brown
damn the soul of a small boy, who had never been baptized
a Christian, after the child accidentally drowned. "Religion's supposed to comfort people, not frighten them to
death!" Cates shouts at the jury in defense of his stance.
Brady's attempts to discredit both Rachel and Cates by
twisting Cates' jibes at Bible stories so that they seem like
angry protests against all forms of religion reach insane
proportions as his tone becomes as wild as that of the Reverend, causing Rachel to burst into tears. Brady is finally

"Sit down, Samson. You're about to get a haircut."

silenced by his wife. Drummond, aware of the damage that
has been done to his client's character, prepares to cross-
examine Rachel, but Cates confounds him by insisting that
he either let her go or he'll change his plea to guilty. Apparently he is beginning to lose faith in his cause, for
Rachel has been siding with her father all this time; she
fails to see why he presses his cause to the extent of making himself a social outcast. However, he still loves her--
as evidenced by his desire to spare her any further mental
torture on the stand.

Desperate for support for his side, Drummond attempts
to call to the stand several experts in the field of biology,
zoology, and geology, but all of them are dismissed by the

judge as irrelevant: "The Bible is on trial here," he pro-
claims. Thoroughly disgusted with the stubbornness and
ignorance of the Hillsboro community, Drummond launches
into a bitter tirade against the repression (exhibited by the
course of the proceedings) of freedom of thought--"which,"
he claims, "is the real issue on trial in this courtroom."
"Ignorance is forever busy and needs feeding," he shouts,
reminding everyone present that as long as people continue
to close their minds to new approaches to learning, "the human race will keep marching backward--BACKWARD--to the
time when men were burned alive for expressing new ideas
for living." His angry words so infuriate the judge that he
moves to hold Drummond in jail in contempt of court. However, a local farmer--the father of the drowned boy, it
turns out--agrees to put up the bail.

Meanwhile, the war against Cates continues in the
city's streets. "We'll hang Bertram Cates from a sour apple
tree; His truth goes marching on!" proclaim the citizens of
Heavenly Hillsboro, holding torches and walking past the jail

Drummond lashes out at Brady as the judge (Harry Morgan)
listens.

where Cates is being held; when he gazes forlornly out his
cell window at the angry protesters below, one of them
throws a bottle at him and nearly knocks out his eye.

Henry Drummond, lying on a bed in his hotel room, is
at odds as to what strategy, if any, to employ next when
Hornbeck throws him a copy of the Bible. As Hornbeck,
holding a drink in either hand, comes toward Drummond, a
look of puzzlement crosses his face as he stares at the old
agnostic clutching the closed book to his chest and grinning
with immense satisfaction. Drummond has had an idea.
Ernest Gold cleverly reprises the "Gimme that ol' time religion" theme from the opening as Kramer fades out and opens
on the Hillsboro courthouse the following morning. Surprising everyone, Drummond calls Brady himself to the stand--a
most unorthodox procedure, as the judge is quick to point
out. Since the judge has ruled Darwin's text inadmissible,
Drummond is left with only one source: the Bible, a subject
on which Brady claims to be an expert. Drummond tries to
get Brady to explain the logic behind some ambiguous biblical phrasing, such as the exact length of the first day of
creation--which, as Brady himself admits, was not governed
by daylight saving time, for the Lord didn't make the sun
until the fourth day. "I do not think about things that ...
I do not think about!" is Brady's reply. "Do you ever
think about things that you do think about?" asks Drummond.
He realizes that he has Brady over a barrel when he coaxes
him into admitting that that first day could have been of in-
definite length. However, Brady continues to content himself with clever, crowd-pleasing phrases such as, "I am more
interested in the Rock of Ages than the age of rocks."
Drummond finally scores his victory when Brady inadvertently declares that only his particular interpretation of the Bible
is correct. Drummond, shouting: "The Gospel according to
Brady! God speaks to Brady, and Brady tells the world!
Brady, Brady, Brady, Almighty!" The spectators raise
their eyebrows in shock as they realize for the first time how
dangerous a conviction of the power of the Scriptures they
have shared with this man for so long.

The interim before the verdict finds Brady for the first
time exhibiting a loss of confidence in his beliefs. "They
[the townsfolk in the courtroom] laughed at me, Mother,"
he sobs while placing his head in his wife's lap like a little
boy. She tells him that she has always been proud of him

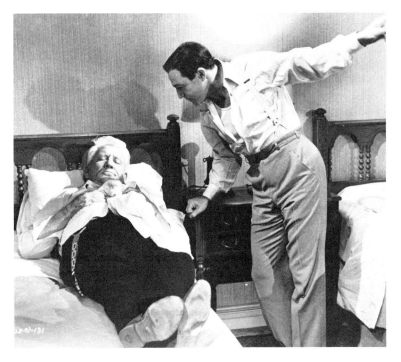

Spencer Tracy and Gene Kelly.

for sticking up for what he believes in, but that "every man has to build his own monument" and commit himself to it without trying to impose his view on others; otherwise, she says, "Yours begins to seem like the only monument worth believing in, and all those who oppose you are wrong." She uses the same reasoning to admonish Rachel, who has come to vent her hostility against her father. "I believe in my husband-- what do you believe in?" she asks Rachel. Rachel eventually returns to the man she loves.

The judge's position is also put to the test the next day in court, when he is warned by one of his associates that his popularity in the upcoming election will be compromised should he impose a strict sentence upon Cates. When the verdict does in fact rule in favor of the prosecution,

the judge merely orders Cates to pay a $100 fine, which
Drummond promptly rejects, stating that he will appeal his
case to the Tennessee Supreme Court. Brady, outraged,
begins spouting some ancient biblical mumbo-jumbo in pro-
test of the too-lenient sentence imposed on Cates, but he
finds that no one is listening. Unable to bear this rejection
and overcome by the sweltering atmosphere of the courtroom,
he faints and dies a few hours later of heart failure.

The last scene finds Drummond and Hornbeck alone in
the courtroom. Hornbeck is busy concocting vicious head-
lines to describe the demise of Brady: "How do you write
an obituary for a man who's been dead thirty years? 'In
Memoriam--M.H.B.' Then what? 'Hail the apostle whose
letters to the Corinthians were lost in the mail'? Why should
we weep for him? He cried enough for himself! The national tear-duct from Weeping Water, Nebraska, who flooded the
whole nation like a one-man Mississippi!" When Drummond
recites verbatim verse 29, Proverbs 11, to give the reason

Brady confronts Rachel.

for Brady's downfall and states that "a giant once lived on
that body, but Matt Brady looked for God too high up and
too far away," Hornbeck immediately pegs him for a Christian: "Excuse me, gentlemen. I must get to a typewriter
and hammer out the story of an atheist who believes in God."
Drummond, steadily losing his patience, replies, "I'm getting
damned tired of you, Hornbeck. You're like a ghost pointing
an empty sleeve at everybody and snickering. Don't you believe in anything? What is your dream? Don't you understand the meaning of what went on here today?" he asks
incredulously. "I tell you Brady had the same right as
Cates: the right to be wrong!" Finally, he reminds Hornbeck pityingly, "You're all alone. Who'll come to your funeral?" For once Hornbeck takes a good look at himself and
is unable to reply--but he manages a final comeback line:
"You'll be there, Henry. Who else would defend my right
to be lonely?" After he leaves, Drummond eyes the copies
of Darwin and the Bible on the bench. He picks one up,
then the other, and looks from one volume to the other,

A beaten Brady with his wife.

balancing them thoughtfully, as if his hands were scales.
He half smiles, half shrugs. Then he slaps the two books
together and jams them in his briefcase, side by side, and
exits the courtroom.

In adapting the stage play to the screen, Nathan E.
Douglas and Harold Jacob Smith have remained faithful to
the text for the most part, although at Kramer's insistence
the larger issue of the story (the right to think, the neces-
sity always to investigate further) was to take precedence
over the singular issue of biblical language and meaning.[3]
The scenarists' main contributions include providing the
Drummond, Hornbeck, and Brady characters with extra
lines of amusement throughout and the rearranging of dia-
logues in order to take advantage of settings outside the
courtroom, thereby de-emphasizing the theatrical nature of
the drama.

Even so, the film (with the exception of the sequences
in the town square) rarely opens out the stage original to
take full advantage of the motion picture camera. Due to
technical necessities, Kramer was forced to keep the entire
trial inside the courtroom. As in Anatomy of a Murder, these
scenes took precedence over the others in the story; they
were the first filmed and were shot in continuity, with
speeches and exchanges photographed in their entirety instead of being broken down into short takes. Fortunately,
this time around Kramer was able to avoid becoming overly
concerned with maintaining visual variety in the courtroom
scenes; however, in his next feature, Judgment at Nuremberg (1961), as we shall see, the task of avoiding a static
element in courtroom sequences became far more difficult,
as over eighty percent of Nuremberg's three-hour running
time was comprised of trial scenes.

In addition, the historical implications of the trial--the
fact that the outcome resulted in the loosening of restrictive
teaching practices in some states, but not Tennessee--take a
back seat in both the film and the play to the histrionics of
the principal players. The dramatizations of the events at
the Scopes Trial were not intended to scrutinize any particular aspect of the judicial process, but were merely stages for
enacting the feud between two colorful and flamboyant personalities; in neither case (play or film) are we as concerned
with their respect for the law as with the drama created by
their courtroom clash of egos.

Nevertheless, as far as the courtroom debate on the issue of evolution versus creation (or, in a broader sense, freedom of thought versus repression of new ideas) is concerned, one can say that Kramer's is a provocative and thought-provoking (though decidedly unsubtle) film which bears his unmistakable mark of sincerity and conviction. Starting with Inherit the Wind and continuing through three subsequent films, one man would remain the spokesman for Kramer's liberal attitudes: Spencer Tracy. Kramer himself told me: "I wasn't taking sides in Inherit the Wind--except I believed Darrow."[4] Even a single viewing of the film will convince the viewer of this: Tracy's presence literally dominates the frame in nearly every scene in which he appears, especially those where he speaks out--not only to the spectators in the courtroom but to the entire audience watching the film--about how "an idea is a greater monument than a cathedral and the advance of man's knowledge is more of a miracle than any sticks turned into snakes or the parting of waters!"

Tracy's standout performance as the wise and woolly Drummond is equally matched by Fredric March's engagingly smug Brady. These two roles are highpoints in the long and distinguished careers of both men. Gene Kelly in the guise of the cynical reporter Hornbeck is something less than perfect, however; his casting in a dramatic role in the film was the result of Kramer's questionable practice of teasing audience expectations by placing a type-cast celebrity in a new and challenging role (recall Fred Astaire as a scientist in On the Beach). Although Kelly gives it a good hard try, he manages to make every witticism sound just a little too pat, a little too studied--and, as one critic quipped, he "seems always to be on the verge of breaking into a little gavotte."[5] Dick York is pretty good as Cates, in a not very well developed characterization, and Florence Eldridge (actually Mrs. Fredric March in real life) lends class and credibility to her scenes with Tracy and with her husband. Harry Morgan also is amusing as the judge.

In all, Inherit the Wind stands today as a handsome (thanks to Ernest Laszlo's ultra-clean cinematography),

---

[Opposite:] Stanley Kramer (center front, squatting, hands clasped) with crew. (Photo courtesy of UCLA film stills archive)

intelligent, and above all engagingly acted adaptation of a
famous stage play--certainly one of the high spots of the
career of its producer-director. As Kramer himself remarked
at the time of its release, the issues raised in the Scopes
trial are timeless:

> It may be thought by some that Darrow's defense of
> Scopes settled the issues of that trial once and for
> all. But this is not the case. The spirit of the
> trial lives on, because the real issues of that trial
> were man's right to teach. These are issues for
> which the never-ending struggle continues, and
> they constitute the real theme of Inherit the Wind.[6]

NOTES

1. Donald Spoto, Stanley Kramer: Film Maker (New York:
   G.P. Putnam's Sons, 1978), pp. 17 and 223.

2. Stanley Kramer, as quoted by Thomas McDonald in
   "Hollywood Trial," New York Times, November 1, 1959.

3. Spoto, p. 219.

4. Letter from Stanley Kramer to author, dated June 17,
   1985.

5. Spoto, p. 220.

6. Spoto, p. 223.

Chapter 7

JUDGMENT AT NUREMBERG

Credits

A Roxlom Production, released through United Artists, 1961.
Producer and Director: Stanley Kramer. Screenplay: Abby
Mann, based on his teleplay of the same name. Director of
Photography: Ernest Laszlo, A.S.C. Editor: Frederic
Knudtson, A.C.E. Music: Ernest Gold. Production De-
signer: Rudolph Sternad. Production Manager: Clem
Beauchamp. Assistant to the Producer: Ivan Volkman.
Sound: James Speak. Associate Producer: Philip Langner.
Wardrobe: Joe King. Miss Dietrich's costumes designed by
Jean Louis. Makeup: Robert J. Schiffer. Set Decorator:
George Milo. Chief Gaffer: Don L. Carstensen. Company
Grip: Morris Rosen. Properties: Art Cole. Assistant
Company Grip: Martin Kashuk. Music Editor: Art Dunham.
Sound Editor: Walter Elliott, M.P.S.E. Song: "Lili Marlene"
--music: Norbert Schultze, lyrics: Hans Leib. Song:
"Liebeslied"--music: Ernest Gold, lyrics: Alfred Perry.
The German Crew: R. Richtsfeld, L. Ostermeier, Lyn
Hannes, Pia Arnold, Albrecht Hennings, Hannelore Winter-
feld, Laci Ronay, Hubert Karl, Eggn Haedler, Frank Water-
stein, R. Eglseder. Casting: Stalmaster-Lister. Titles by
Pacific Title. Black-and-white. Running Time: 178 minutes.

Cast: Spencer Tracy (Judge Dan Haywood), Burt Lancaster
(Ernst Janning), Richard Widmark (Col. Tad Lawson), Marlene Dietrich (Mme. Bertholt), Maximilian Schell (Hans Rolfe),

129

Judy Garland (Irene Hoffman), Montgomery Clift (Rudolf
Petersen), William Shatner (Capt. Byers), Edward Binns
(Senator Burkette), Kenneth MacKenna (Judge Kenneth Nor-
ris), Werner Klemperer (Emil Hahn), Torben Meyer (Werner
Lammpe), Alan Baxter (Gen. Merrin), Ray Teal (Judge Cur-
tis Ives), Martin Brandt (Friedrich Hofstetter), Virginia
Christine (Mrs. Halbestadt), Ben Wright (Mr. Halbestadt),
Joseph Bernard (Major Abe Radnitz), John Wengraf (Dr.
Wieck), Karl Swenson (Dr. Geuter), Howard Caine (Wallner),
Otto Waldis (Pohl), Olga Fabian (Mrs. Lindnow), Sheila Brom-
ley (Mrs. Ives), Bernard Kates (Perkins), Jana Taylor (Elsa
Scheffler), Paul Busch (Schmidt).

        In 1961 the Nazi War Crimes Trials were still an un-
popular subject among Americans and Germans alike, even
though the trials were originally conducted back in the late
1940s. For those individuals who still held harrowing memories of German concentration camps, the idea of resurrect-
ing long-buried (and painfully so) issues seemed almost un-
thinkable at this point in time, particularly in light of the
disturbing truth that few of the criminals originally sentenced were still serving time in prison.

        However, there was one man in Hollywood who thought
differently: Stanley Kramer. "It can never be too early or
too late for a film of the war crimes trials. Mengele--dead
or alive?" was Kramer's response when the author posed that
question to him. After all, he had reasoned, Abby Mann's
teleplay Judgment at Nuremberg, which concerned a fictionalized trial of Nazi judges for crimes against humanity, had
lured huge audiences when it had aired on TV's Playhouse
90 in April 1959. Also--and more importantly--this was to
be perhaps Kramer's most personal film, a "sort of summary
of my work,"[1] referring to the picture's main concern, for
"truth, justice and the value of a single human being."
Commenting further on his intentions behind adapting the
play to the screen, Kramer told me, "Nuremberg certainly
expressed my own feelings--as well as being a prod to Americans and Germans to remember what had happened."[2]

        Unfortunately, United Artists, the distributor of all of
Kramer's five previous films as producer/director, did not
share his enthusiasm at first. Kramer told Spoto: "Do you
think [they] wanted to get involved in a film about war

trials? They weren't interested at all in war guilt, people
in ovens, or crooked judges. 'That's a courtroom thing,'
they said, 'and besides, no one knows who the protagonists
are!' So what I did was something of a compromise: I stud-
ded it with stars to get it made as a film that would reach
out to a mass audience, made in America at the prices necessary to pay here."[3] Hence the presence of Judy Garland in
a small dramatic role (recall Gene Kelly in Kramer's Inherit
the Wind, released the previous year) and the likes of Spencer
Tracy, Burt Lancaster, Marlene Dietrich, Richard Widmark,
and Montgomery Clift heading the large cast. In addition,
although Kramer was able to utilize the authentic Nuremberg
locations for the exteriors, the most frequently seen locale,
that of the courtroom, was still being used at the time,
so, Kramer said, "We took measurements and carefully re-
created it on the soundstage in Hollywood, although we
finally had to scale down some of the dimensions for the
involved camera movements."[4]

Abby Mann's screenplay, like his teleplay, concerns
itself solely with the second Nuremberg trials, where judges
were the defendants. However, it must be emphasized that
although, as Kramer says, "the testimony came out of trial
manuscript and is a fact of the postwar attitudes,"[5] the
film "is not a documentation of actual facts and names but
a fictional composite ... Instead of treating the actual historical situation of ... twenty-two defendants," the story
presents "a quartet of Nazi judges as the sole defendants,"
and as a result, as Donald Spoto points out, "the issue
is focused and becomes the judgment of justice, and the
theme of the corruptibility of the legal system is thus thrown
into greater relief."[6]

Kramer informed me that although he and Abby Mann
were dealing with issues of considerable moral and social
depth, their film "was not aimed at a specifically intellectual
audience--but to everyone." Donald Spoto's statement that
their main concern was to "reflect on and understand"[7] the
period during which the trials occurred could not have been
more accurate: there is scarcely a moment in the film's
three hours when the viewer does not sense that Kramer
and his whole crew have made every effort possible to create a feeling of empathy for the characters involved and the
times in which they are living.

Judge Haywood (Spencer Tracy) in Nuremberg. (Photo
courtesy of Museum of Modern Art/Film Stills Archive)

        Occasionally, however, the results are somewhat ques-
tionable: the four-minute overture--comprised of slowly
rising Nazi "heils"--which precedes the credits, for example,
seems little more than an irritating delay; it is usually de-
leted when the film is shown on television. The credits
themselves, however, are inventive: a swastika is formed
piece-by-piece with a new actor's name appearing with each
successive segment until the puzzle is completed and the
swastika spins out of sight, becoming the emblem on top of
Hitler's infamous stadium as the black background of the titles dissolves. At the close of the credit music, the emblem
explodes, signaling the fact that the Nazi Reign of Terror
has ended. A subtitle informs us that we are in Nuremberg,
Germany, in the year 1948. After a slow pan across the
ruins of the city, we discover Judge Dan Haywood (Spencer
Tracy) being chauffeured to his temporary quarters where
he will reside while presiding over the Nuremberg trials.

He is irritated by the arrogant demeanor of the German
driver, who insists on honking his horn whenever possible
in an attempt to assert the dignity of his people, which has
obviously taken a beating since the truths about the concentration camps were exposed. We will see many more ex-
amples of such attitudes as the film progresses.

Haywood, we soon discover, is a backwoods judge
from Maine who was recently defeated for re-election there.
A basically simple man in terms of lifestyle, he feels ill at
ease with the elaborate quarters which have been assigned
him and with the overly obliging attitudes of the servants,
Mr. and Mrs. Halbestadt (Ben Wright and Virginia Christine).
"I think the whole state of Maine would be comfortable here,"
he remarks with playful yet sincere dissatisfaction. Haywood
may come from unsophisticated surroundings, but he is no
fool: "I wasn't the first choice for this position, and you
know it," he tells one of his attendants. Nevertheless, despite the unpopularity of the trials, he feels they should go
on and he will try his best to uphold the position to which
he has been assigned. At this point he is as puzzled as
any outsider as to how men of such esteemed reputations as
the judges on trial could have sent so many innocent people
to die. Throughout the course of the trial, he will remain
the audience's link to understanding the complexities of the
issues discussed; indeed, this is what Kramer intended, for
Tracy's presence in this film, more than in any of Kramer's
others, is used as a vehicle for voicing the director's most
personal views on the nature of human existence.

At the start of the trial, three of the judges in the
dock plead guilty, but one, Ernst Janning (Burt Lancaster),
refuses to enter a plea because he does not acknowledge
the authority of the tribunal. The American prosecuting
attorney, Col. Tad Lawson (Richard Widmark) opens his
address by lashing out at the defendants, emphasizing that
they were not naive youngsters but rather educated adults
when they agreed to side with Hitler. Lawson, who has
been dealing with Nazi criminals for the past two years, has
grown increasingly hostile in his attitude toward them.
"Here they'll receive the justice they denied others," he
declares, obviously intent upon obtaining the maximum punishment for the judges. The attorney for the defense, Hans
Rolfe (Maximilian Schell), counters by pointing out that if
the judges in the dock are guilty, then so is all of Germany:

"A judge does not make the laws; he merely carries them out," he says. This is the crux of the proceedings: are judges who administer laws they did not make responsible for the cruelties and injustices those laws engender?

Ernst Janning, as Judge Haywood discovers after reading some of his books, was a highly respected and learned man who inexplicably agreed in the prewar years to a temporary suspension of justice. At this point, Haywood is willing to accept Hans Rolfe's explanation that Janning knew nothing of the atrocities which were taking place during his period in office.

Kramer and Mann strongly hint that the administering of a truly unbiased verdict will ultimately rest with Judge Haywood alone. Haywood is the only one of the three presiding judges who is eager to look beyond superficial evidence; the other two are not interested in the human side of Ernst Janning (as evidenced in his writings), but rather

Haywood and Mme. Bertholt (Marlene Dietrich). (Photo courtesy of Museum of Modern Art/Film Stills Archive)

with the objective facts of the case alone. While they spend
the weekends with family and friends, Haywood takes in the
sights and sounds of Nuremberg in an attempt to determine
the attitudes of the German people toward the events that
took place during Hitler's reign. However, when he tries to
question Mr. and Mrs. Halbestadt, his two servants, as to
what it was like living under National Socialism, he encount-
ers a sudden hushed attitude and an abundance of denials
as to their knowledge that any of the infamous activities--
such as imprisonment of millions of Jews and others in concentration camps--were occurring. Their facade of innocence
is embarrassingly betrayed when Mr. Halbestadt blurts out,
"But if we did know--what could we do?"

Haywood's suspicion that the majority of Germans would
rather forget the past than try to face it is confirmed when
he meets Madame Bertholt (Marlene Dietrich), the aristocratic
widow of a German officer executed after the first war crimes
trials. "Hitler hated me, Ernst Janning, and my husband,"
she tells him, emphasizing her husband's devotion to duty
and ignoring the crimes of which he was a part. "You have
to understand--me, my husband, we did not know of those
things--only Hitler and Goebbels and a few others were aware
they were going on." "I don't know what to think," Haywood
snaps bitterly. "As far as I can make out, no one knew
anything." "We have to forget if we are to go on living,"
she tells Haywood, at which point Kramer cuts to beer steins
being banged on tables in a pub as a patriotic hymn is sung.

Back in court, meanwhile, Col. Lawson, in an attempt
to support his accusations of the inhuman acts perpetrated
by Janning and others, offers the testimony of Rudolf Petersen (Montgomery Clift), a middle-aged baker's assistant who
was judged mentally incompetent by the Nazis and therefore
sterilized for the good of the country. Rolfe shrewdly attempts to prove to the tribunal that Petersen's feeble-
mindedness is a congenital condition and that his steriliza-
tion was justified. He produces evidence of Petersen's un-
satisfactory performance on intelligence tests in school and
tries to get him to take a similar test in the courtroom,
which he ignores, emphasizing that "they [the Nazi officials]
had already made up their minds before I ever got to the
hospital [for tests]. I was not feeble-minded!" At any
rate, Judge Haywood is deeply moved by the plight of this
obviously unstable man, a victim of Nazi tortures.

Maximilian Schell as Hans Rolfe.

Col. Lawson is certain that he will be able to win over
the support of the tribunal when he hears that a Jewish
woman named Irene Hoffman is in Nuremberg. After much
persuasion, Hoffman (Judy Garland), a middle-aged hausfrau,
agrees to give up the privacy she has established and come
to the trial. She testifies that when she was thirteen an
elderly Jewish friend of hers named Feldenstein was wrongly
accused (by Emil Hahn, one of the judges in the dock) of
being intimate with her (thereby "polluting the Aryan race")
and then executed. When Rolfe tries to break down her
story by falsely accusing her of distorting the truth, the
distraught woman breaks down into hysterical denials.
Ernst Janning, who has remained silent thus far, then interrupts the proceedings and asks to make a statement.
"Are we going to do this again?" he asks Rolfe, referring
to the story of the "sacrificial ritual" in which "Feldenstein
the Jew was the helpless victim." The point, he says, is not
whether the man was guilty but that Aryan sexual relations
with Jews was immoral. In his subsequent speech he traces

Burt Lancaster as Ernst Janning.

the subversion of justice in his court to the spirit of national pride which the German people, in a time of emotional and spiritual crisis, had adopted from Hitler:

> It is not easy to tell the truth, but if there is to be any salvation for Germany, we who know our guilt must admit it.... My counsel would have you believe we were not aware of the concentration camps. Not aware?! Where were we?! ... My counsel says we were not aware of the extermination of the millions. He would give you the excuse that we were only aware of the extermination of the hundreds. Does that make us any the less guilty? Maybe we didn't know the details. But if we didn't know, it was because we didn't <u>want</u> to know ... Ernst Janning [was] worse than any of [the corrupt judges] because he knew what they were, and he went along with them.[8]

Needless to say, this speech has a great impact upon Judge Haywood, for now he is finally beginning to understand --much to his horror--how such monstrous acts could be equated with a man as revered as Janning. His picture of Janning as a corrupt figure is reinforced by Col. Lawson's presentation of actual concentration camp footage, showing the infamous gas ovens and hundreds upon hundreds of bodies being bulldozed. Indeed, as Spoto points out, "This was a bold stroke by Kramer, since this of course tends to reduce to insignificance everything else in the film and to make this film within a film the most memorable element"[9]-- although the word "memorable" is certainly devoid of all pleasurable connotations in this context. Kramer inserts many reaction shots of Haywood during this scene to emphasize his gradual comprehension of and growing resentment toward the acts of which the men in the dock were obviously a part.

In his closing address, Hans Rolfe, in an attempt to recover from the shattering revelations of Janning's speech, points out that Janning was instrumental in preventing the executions of many persons. "I want to leave the German people their dignity," he says. "If we are to survive, we must look to the future" (recall Mme. Bertholt's statement). Finally, he states that if Ernst Janning is to be found guilty, so must others. He reminds Haywood and the other judges

Richard Widmark as Col. Lawson, the American prosecutor.

that as late as 1937 "The Russians signed pacts with Hitler,
Churchill praised him, American industrialists profited by
him.... Ernst Janning's guilt is the world's guilt. No
more, no less."

Before Haywood and the other two judges, Norris
(Kenneth MacKenna) and Ives (Ray Teal), are permitted to
reach a decision, however, Mann throws a monkey wrench
into the path of justice: it seems that both the American
Judge Haywood and the German Judge Janning are faced
with the question of whether to submit to political pressure
from governments who see the outcome of the trials in terms
of political expediency. The trials take place during the
Berlin crisis of 1948, as American troops airlift supplies to
Berlin. The American military occupation government fore-
sees the need for a German ally in the face of a Russian
threat, and they are therefore anxious to avoid antagonizing
their ally with the Nuremberg trials. The German judges

were only upholding their country's laws, argues the American military. Besides, as one senator remarks, "The American public isn't interested in the outcome of the Nuremberg trials anyway." General Matt Merrin, a longtime friend of Col. Lawson, points out to him the logic of "going easy" on the judges. "You don't get the support of the German people by sentencing their leaders to stiff prison sentences," he reminds him. "After all, isn't survival at any cost the most important thing?" he asks, to which Lawson replies with bitterness, "Just for laughs, Matt--what was the war all about?" Lawson's closing remarks, however, reveal that he has given into the pressure but that it remains to be seen whether Judge Haywood and the others will allow concern for political expediency to stand in the way of the administration of justice. "Such is the dilemma of our times," Lawson concludes.

Judy Garland as Irene Hoffman.

Montgomery Clift as Rudolf Petersen.

Judge Haywood eventually finds all four defendants--
Janning included--guilty of deliberately committing crimes
against humanity "in violation of every moral and legal
principle known to all civilized nations" and sentences them
to life imprisonment. However, he agrees with Rolfe that
indeed there are others who must share the ultimate responsibility for what happened in Germany. "The real complain-
ing party at the bar in this courtroom is civilization," he
reminds everyone present.

> Ernst Janning, to be sure, is a tragic figure. We
> believe he loathed the evil he did. But compassion
> for the present torture of his soul must not beget
> forgetfulness of the torture and death of millions
> by the government of which he was a part. Jan-
> ning's record and his fate illuminate the most shat-
> tering truth that has emerged from this trial: if
> he and the other defendants were all degraded

perverts--if all the leaders of the Third Reich were
sadistic monsters--then these events would have no
more moral significance than an earthquake, or any
other natural catastrophe. But this trial has shown
that under a national crisis, able--even able and
extraordinary men--can delude themselves into the
commission of crimes so vast and heinous that they
beggar the imagination.... There are those in our
own country, too, who today speak of the protec-
tion of country. Of survival. A decision must be
made. In the life of every divilized nation, at the
very moment when the grasp of the enemy is at
its throat, then it seems that the only way to survive is to use the means of the enemy, to rest survival upon what is expedient, to look the other way.
Only--the answer to that is: survival as what? A
country isn't a rock. It's never the extension of
one's self--it's what it stands for. It's what it
stands for when standing for something is the most
difficult. Before the people of the world--let it now
be noted that here in our decision this is what we
stand for--Justice, Truth ... and the value of a
single human being.[10]

Again, as in Inherit the Wind, Spencer Tracy speaks not
only to the spectators in the courtroom, but to the viewing
audience--and, in a broader sense, to the whole world.

The next morning, as Haywood is preparing to return
to the United States, he is met by Rolfe, who says he would
like to make a wager with him: he bets that in five years'
time all of the defendants whom Haywood sentenced will have
been set free. Haywood defiantly replies, "I don't make
wagers. What you say may very well come to pass, in light
of the world situation today. Your powers of logic never
cease to amaze me, Hans Rolfe, but to be logical is not to
be right."

Before Haywood departs, he stops by Janning's cell,
at his request. Janning gives him some records of the trial
that he has been keeping and says that he respects the tribunal's decision but asks whether Haywood can personally
understand why he complied with the Nazi laws. Referring
to all the subsequent atrocities, Janning says, "I did not
know it would come to that. You must believe it." Haywood

responds, much to Janning's surprise, "It came to that the
very first time you sentenced to death a man you knew to
be innocent." He then walks solemnly out of the jail, and
we are reminded of the exit of the same actor from the Hillsboro Courthouse at the conclusion of Inherit the Wind. A
final title informs us that Rolfe's predictions were more than
prophetic: of the ninety-nine men sentenced to life imprisonment during the Nuremberg trials, not one is still serving
time.

According to Donald Spoto, "The Nuremberg trials were
very different from what is here represented. Judges were
not defendants in them--politicians were, as well as government, navy and army officials, Gestapo leaders and SS (elite
guard) officials.... Also, there were no women witnesses at
these trials, and although the real-life basis for the judge
portrayed by Tracy was indeed an American (Francis Biddle
of Massachusetts), there were also Russian, British and
French presiding judges; here all three are Americans. In
addition, the actual trials convicted twenty-two men, of whom
twelve were sentenced to hang, three to life imprisonment,
two to twenty years, one each to fifteen and ten years, and
three acquitted."[11] Also, referring to the issue of political
expediency involving the cold war, Spoto remarks, "Things
never got this obvious or dramatic: the military commander
of American forces in Germany at the time, John J. McCloy,
did suggest that harsh verdicts might have new, unforeseen
ramifications, but no such political consideration ever weighed
in the final sentences, as the record indicates."[12]

Kramer's obligation to respect the formal atmosphere of
the courtroom at Nuremberg (where attorneys were kept at
all times a certain specified distance from the defendants and
where all involved remained permanently stationary) obviously
posed a problem in terms of avoiding staticness in these sequences. He was not permitted the attention to detail that
Preminger exhibited in Anatomy of a Murder; the camera had
to remain focused on the speaker at the podium, and the
attorneys who remained seated could not exhibit quaint little
habits such as fiddling with pills (Sir Wilfrid Robarts in
Witness for the Prosecution) or fish hooks (Paul Biegler in
Anatomy) to help them pass the time. Also, there is (appropriately) very little humor in the film, although Tracy's
wanderings around Nuremberg are always engaging (at one
point he stops to buy a frankfurter from a young woman

Judge Haywood makes his plea for "Justice, Truth, and the value of a single human being."

who, much to his surprise, greets him with "Hello, grandpa."). The most effective moment of tension-reduction in the courtroom sequences comes when Rolfe, preoccupied with embarrassing Rudolf Petersen on the stand, asks him what he told the Nazis when they questioned him as to his knowledge of the birthdates of Hitler and Goebbels, and Petersen replies, "I told them I didn't know and, what's more, that I didn't <u>care</u> when they were born," which elicits a hearty chuckle from the spectators.

Referring to the difficulties of avoiding stasis in the unusually restricted courtroom settings, Kramer remarked to Spoto: "The film becomes a ping-pong game unless you try to move the camera, which I tried--not always successfully-- to do."[13] Often during the characters' speeches, to provide fluidity and prevent boredom, Kramer will circle the courtroom

completely in an attempt to catch the reactions of the judges
and the spectators to what is being said. His slow pans
serve the function of taking up the time needed for the
lengthy cross-examinations--and also seem much more natural
and logical than the use of extreme closeups, which have a
tendency to insult the viewer by limiting his perspective
(even Preminger, the reader will recall, managed to avoid
them unless absolutely necessary during the long, unbroken
scenes in the courtroom in Anatomy). Kramer's glides
around the courtroom are fairly unobtrusive for the most
part, but this technique tends to wear thin when stretched
over three solid hours of running time. Ultimately, the
courtroom sequences amount to little more than talky (although highly intriguing) marathons. At least in Anatomy
Wendell Mayes was always able to provide the viewer with
exciting entertainment on the surface while at the same time
managing to make numerous statements about the nature of
the judicial system.

There is also a problem, as one critic at the time of
the film's United States release (December 1961) pointed out,
with pacing: "There is a lack of a sense of time passing,
for this trial is said to have consumed eight months."[14]
While Kramer deserves much credit for spacing out the
courtroom scenes in such a manner as to avoid overwhelming
the viewer with the issues (the speeches are knocked off in
swift strokes and there is usually not more than one preceding
a scene with a character outside of court), he has, in the
process, failed to instill a sense of vicariousness in the
viewer: at the end of the film, despite the fact that the
viewer has been watching for three solid hours, he does not
feel as exhausted as he should because he has not, as he
would be required to do in Anatomy, sat through the courtroom sequences without a break. However, in this case, if
the many lengthy speeches without character movement were
lumped together, the effect would most likely serve to put
the viewer to sleep, no matter how stimulating the discussion.
Even as the film stands, as Variety's critic put it, "It is a
heavy, demanding attraction that requires unusually deep
and sustained concentration, perhaps more than most modern
audiences will be willing to give."[15]

Apparently he was right: Judgment at Nuremberg was
a resounding flop at the box office. This fact could also
probably be attributed to its being released during the

Christmas-New Year's season, a time when light entertainments seem most popular with the public. Nevertheless,
Kramer's attitude toward this unfavorable reception by German as well as American audiences--the film premiered in
Berlin in October 1961 to crowds of shocked citizens who
did not appreciate his rehashing of one of the most shameful
periods in German history--remains refreshingly sincere:
"Nuremberg's box-office result was disappointing to me because I knew better than most that when you fail to reach a
mass audience it is the fault of the film, not the audience."

Critical response was greatly varied. Those who liked
the film were apparently more concerned with Kramer's intentions and presentation of important issues than with the
film's dramatic merits: it was hailed as an "event," an "experience." Those who opposed it quickly grew impatient
with its incessant talkiness and as a result labeled it
"preachy." Nor was their anger tempered by Abby
Mann's acceptance of an Academy Award for Best Screenplay Adaptation "on behalf of all intellectuals." Kramer,
however, has a pat rebuttal for those critics: "Preachy?
I think not. It points a finger at those who insist nobody
knew what was going on--yet tries to comprehend they were
human beings--Schell, Dietrich, the Halbestadts, Lancaster."
Kramer's judgment is ultimately more accurate: he and Mann
have presented their issues in so remarkably clear a fashion
and with such overwhelming conviction that it is hard to
condemn the film for robbing the viewer of his self-respect.

Critic Brendan Gill's snide description of the film as
an "all-star concentration-camp drama with special guest-
victim appearances"[16] may have some surface relevance with
regard to Kramer's choices of Judy Garland and Montgomery
Clift to fill roles that would normally have been given to un-
knowns. However, once one gets over the shock of seeing
Garland portraying a German (she certainly doesn't look like
one, despite her padding) he will find that she--and Clift--
are quite affecting in their portrayals of shaken victims of
Nazi atrocities. Additional sympathy is elicited for Clift
when one realizes that he agreed to play the part during a
very traumatic period in his life: he had recently been
severely scarred in an automobile accident. As Kramer told
Spoto: "I had to bolster his confidence all the time."[17]
Burt Lancaster's role as the stoical defendant Janning was
too confining for this physically-oriented actor. This is not

to say, however, that he could not be effective in a basically subdued role; he proved he could and then some the following year as prisoner Robert Stroud in John Frankenheimer's Birdman of Alcatraz. Richard Widmark at first seems a bit overzealous in his desire to see that justice is done to the judges on trial, but in light of the later revelations the viewer, along with Judge Haywood, comes to appreciate his anger. Marlene Dietrich is elegant and refined in every way as the aristocratic Mme. Bertholt. This was her first dramatic role since Witness for the Prosecution, and she outclasses her performance in that film by a mile. Maximilian Schell won the Best Actor Academy Award for his masterful portrayal (an extension of his role in the TV version of the story) of the defense lawyer Rolfe, with his disturbing tic-like smile and cunning demeanor. And finally there is Spencer Tracy, giving one of his last great performances as the decent, humane superjudge who must render a monumental decision. He provides a perfect model through whom the audience can come to grips with the conflicting issues which the film raises. Kramer's characteristic modesty shone through when he commented upon his direction of Tracy: "He and I had such a rapport that I am sure we affected each other--he as a great actor and I with the desire to put him--and the philosophy--on film."

Also contributing to the film's overall impact are the stark, authentic-looking cinematography of Ernest Laszlo (who had earlier photographed Kramer's Inherit the Wind [1960] and who would again assist him on It's a Mad, Mad, Mad, Mad World [1963] and Ship of Fools [1965]) and the score of Ernest Gold, composed largely of authentic Nazi marches and hymns.

In the final analysis, Judgment at Nuremberg stands today as one of the strongest and most memorable courtroom dramas in terms of its honest, straightforward presentation and because of the impact of its messages--most notably Tracy's statement concerning "Justice, Truth and the value of a single human being." Though it is not a documentation of a real trial but rather a fictionalized composite, as mentioned earlier, its fidelity to the conduct of the actual Nuremberg trials (if not always to the facts) and the conviction with which its ideas are put across help to place it above its director's previous effort, Inherit the Wind (1960), and to make it his most personal achievement. However, in light of

the (unavoidable) talkiness of the courtroom scenes, it
would seem that the discussion of its issues might be better
suited to a less taxing format--a formal debate, for example.
Clearly, as Kramer himself has said, its messages are timeless and must be re-examined continually if we are to prevent the recurrence of the events which took place during
that fateful period in history. Indeed, such an attitude
motivated him to undertake the project in the first place.

NOTES

1. Donald Spoto, Stanley Kramer: Film Maker (New York:
    G.P. Putnam's Sons, 1978), p. 225.

2. Letter from Stanley Kramer to author, dated June 17,
    1985.

3. Spoto, p. 229.

4. Spoto, p. 229.

5. Kramer letter.

6. Spoto, p. 226.

7. Spoto, p. 226.

8. Abby Mann, Judgment at Nuremberg (London: Cassell
    & Co., Ltd., 1961), p. 169.

9. Spoto, p. 226.

10. Mann, pp. 169-171.

11. Spoto, p. 228.

12. Spoto, p. 230.

13. Spoto, p. 229.

14. Hollis Alpert, review of Nuremberg in Saturday Review,
     December 2, 1961.

15. "Tube," review of Nuremberg in Variety, October 18,
     1961.

16. Brendan Gill as quoted by Pauline Kael in 5001 Nights
     at the Movies (New York: Holt, Rinehart and Winston,
     1982), p. 294.

17. Spoto, p. 233.

Chapter 8

THE VERDICT

Credits

A Zanuck/Brown Production, released through 20th Century-Fox, 1982. Co-producers: Richard D. Zanuck and David Brown. Director: Sidney Lumet. Screenplay: David Mamet, based upon the novel by Barry Reed. Director of Photography: Andrzej Bartkowiak. Editor: Peter Frank. Music: Johnny Mandel. Production Designer: Edward Prisoni. Costume Design: Anna Hill Johnstone. Executive Producer: Burtt Harris. Unit Production Manager: Joseph M. Caracciolo. First Assistant Director: Burtt Harris. Second Assistant Director: Robert E. Warren. Unit Manager: Jennifer M. Ogden. Script Supervisor: Kay Chapin. Camera Operator: William Steiner. Assistant Cameramen: Hank and Gary Muller. Second Assistant Cameraman: Bob Paone. Stillman: Louis Goldman. Sound Mixer: James Sabat. Boom Men: Louis Sabat, Frank Graziadei. Art Director: John Kasarda. Set Director: George DeTitta. Scenic Artists: Edward Garzero, William Sohmer. Prop Master: Joseph Caracciolo, Jr. Props: John McDonnell. Set Dresser: David Weinman. Gaffer: Dusty Wallace. Key Grip: Bobby Ward. Dolly Grip: Eddie Quinn. Construction Foreman: Carlos Quiles, Sr. Construction Grip: Joe Williams, Sr. Wardrobe: Marilyn Putnam, Bill Loger. Makeup Artists: Joe Cranzano, Monty Westmore. Hair Stylist: Bob Grimaldi. DGA Trainee: Ken Ornstein. Production Office Coordinator: Eileen Eichenstein. Transportation Captain: James Fanning. Assistant to Mr. Lumet:

Lilith Jacobs. Production Assistants: Sally Brim, Todd
Winters. Production Auditor: Kathleen McGill, Production
Services, Ltd. Unit Publicist: Ellen Levene. Sound Edi-
tors: Lon Cerborino, Maurice Schell. Assistant Editor:
Andrew Mondschein. Apprentice Editor: David Gelfand.
Music Engineer: Joel Moss. Re-recording Mixer: Lee
Dichten. Locations: Chris Stola, Alexandra Decker. Ti-
tles by R. Greenburg Associates, Inc. Casting: Jay Todd,
Inc. Boston Casting: The Casting Company. Panavision.
De-Luxe. Running Time: 128 minutes.

Cast: Paul Newman (Frank Galvin), Charlotte Rampling
(Laura Fischer), Jack Warden (Mickey Morrissey), James
Mason (Ed Concannon), Milo O'Shea (Judge Hoyle), Edward
Binns (Bishop Brophy), Julie Bovasso (Maureen Rooney),
Lindsay Crouse (Kaitlin Costello Price), Roxanne Hart (Sally
Doneghy), James Handy (Dick Doneghy), Wesley Addy (Dr.
Towler), Lewis Stadlen (Dr. Gruber), Kent Broadhurst
(Joseph Alito), Colin Stinton (Billy), Burtt Harris (Jimmy),
Scott Rhyne (Young Priest), Susan Benenson (Deborah Ann
Kaye), Evelyn Moore (Gruber's Nurse), Juanita Fleming
(Gruber's Maid), Jack Colland (Bailiff), Ralph Douglas
(Clerk), Gregor Roy (Jury Foreman), John Blood (Funeral
Director), Dick McGoldrick (Manager/2nd Funeral Parlor),
Edward Mason (Widow's Son), Patty O'Brien (Irish Nurse 1),
Maggie Task (Irish Nurse 2), Joseph Bergman (Friedman),
Herbert Rubens (Abrams), J.R. Foley (John, Cigar Stand),
Leib Lensky (Wheelchair Patient), Clay Dear (Courthouse
lawyer), J.J. Clark (Courthouse Guard), Greg Doucette
(Sheraton Bar Waiter), Tony LaFortezza (Sheraton Bartend-
er), Marvin Beck, Herb Peterson (Sheraton Bar Patrons).

During the decade stretching from the mid-1960s to
the mid-1970s, the courtroom drama virtually vanished from
sight. Preoccupation with the war in Vietnam and with the
search for identity and freedom of sexual expression was
characteristic of American films made during this period.
Pictures like Dennis Hopper's Easy Rider (1969), Mike Nichols'
The Graduate (1967) and Carnal Knowledge (1971), and Bob
Rafelson's Five Easy Pieces (1970), most of which dealt with
the exploits of society's deviants, quickly became popular
hits, especially among young people, who now comprised the
majority of audiences at theaters across the country.

Concern with the growing crime rates in the nation's

major cities (New York in particular) was responsible for the huge box-office returns of films like Francis Ford Coppola's The Godfather (1972) and its sequel, The Godfather, Part II (1974), Don Siegel's Dirty Harry (1971), and Michael Winner's Death Wish (1974). In addition, there cropped up during this period a rash of largely second-rate disaster epics (1969's Airport and its three clones, Airport '75, '77 and '79, Poseidon Adventure [1972] and Towering Inferno [1974]).

At any rate, it seemed that the heyday of the American courtroom film remained firmly rooted in the 1950s and 1960s. Sidney J. Furie's The Lawyer, released in 1970, proved to be little more than a mildly diverting exploration of issues covered much more professionally in Anatomy of a Murder. Nineteen-seventy-nine's inane satire on the workings of justice, And Justice for All, hardly served to rejuvenate interest in the genre either.

However, 1982 saw the release of a formidable contender with the courtroom dramas of old, The Verdict. Coincidentally, the project reunited three members of the 12 Angry Men crew: actors Jack Warden and Edward Binns and director Sidney Lumet. No doubt what attracted Lumet to the prospect of making a film based on Barry Reed's popular novel about a trial for medical negligence was its theme of the loner versus society, which Lumet had explored at several earlier points in his career, beginning with 12 Angry Men back in 1957, as we have seen, and continuing through the next two decades with The Pawnbroker (1965), Serpico (1973), and Dog Day Afternoon (1975). The Verdict, which concerns the rehabilitation of a has-been Boston lawyer, may most profitably be discussed by comparison with Anatomy of a Murder. As we shall see, the two films share many of the same concerns about the workings of the judicial process.

Lumet establishes the character of his protagonist, Frank Galvin (Paul Newman), in the opening shots. We see a studied profile of a darkened figure staring down at a noisy pinball machine (there is no music during the credits, only the ping-ping of the machine) and, behind him, a well-structured window frame which separates him from the rest of the world. Alone, isolated, and passive, he loses the game, drinks his beer, and lets life amble past. We soon discover that Frank had once been a promising young

attorney, married to the wealthy daughter of his employer,
whose law-school idealism had led him to become the victim
of a crooked judge who accused him (wrongly) of jury tampering and had him thrown in jail, with the result that he
was nearly disbarred. Now, some four years later, he has
been reduced to the status of an ambulance-chaser, begging
funeral-home operators to let him pass his cards to the be-
reaved.

Galvin is busy stumbling about his office in his usual
drunken stupor one day when he is visited by his friend and
former mentor, Mickey Morrissey (Jack Warden), the only individual remaining from Frank's past who will still have anything to do with him. Mickey reminds his old buddy "Frankie" about a case involving a malpractice suit against a Roman
Catholic hospital in Boston which Frank had agreed to take
on over a year and a half ago, but which he had, not sur-
prisingly, forgotten about. It seems that a court date is
finally imminent. Mickey, who is thoroughly disgusted with
the state to which his friend has degenerated, warns him,
"I'm through fuckin' with you, Frankie. It's up to you to
make something of yourself."

Apparently the force of Mickey's words has penetrated
Frank's alcohol-soaked brain, for we next find him straight-
ening up his office in an attempt to look respectable for his
clients, the sister and brother-in-law of the subject of the
dispute, a young woman named Deborah Ann Kaye who was
rendered irreversibly blind, paralyzed, and comatose when
doctors failed to anesthetize her properly during childbirth.
The woman's relatives, anxious to move out West and forget
the ordeal they've suffered for the past four years, are relieved to hear Frank say that the case has very little chance
of ever getting to court. Frank's main concern is with col-
lecting his third of the hefty sum which an out-of-court settlement promises. Again, as in Anatomy, we are shown that
people's personal motives govern their actions. Both Frank
and the Doneghys, the relatives, are more concerned with
how they themselves will benefit from taking the easy way
out--settling out-of-court--than with the welfare of the victim.

Everything proceeds smoothly at first. Frank even
secures the promise of a deposition from a Doctor Gruber
stating that Kaye suffered brain damage from swallowing her

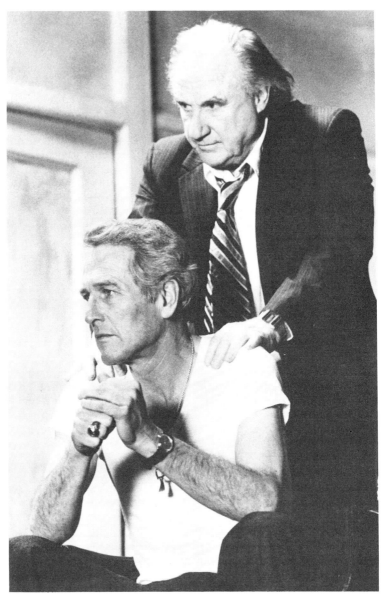

Frank (Paul Newman) and his old buddy Mickey (Jack Warden).

own vomit as the result of receiving an anesthetic shortly
after eating--an illegal medical procedure. However, when
Frank visits the hospital a second time with the intent of
taking some photos of the victim in order to lend extra
sympathy to his side--and thereby raising the amount of
the settlement--he begins to experience a change of heart.
Here Lumet makes inspired use of the Polaroid camera: as
Frank watches the pictures develop, he begins to see and
understand for the first time the tragic results of two doctors' negligence: the utter helplessness of this once-active
individual--"one of the weak," as he says, "who has no one
to fight for her." Significantly, his reply to a nurse who
asks that he leave the ward is, "I'm her attorney."

Frank next meets the Bishop of the Archdiocese (Edward Binns) which controls the Boston hospital where the
girl was treated. The Bishop, claiming that Kaye's situation
is "unfortunate" and that "there is nothing we can do to
make her well again," and anxious to avoid public embarrass-
ment should the case get to court, offers Frank a check from
the church's law firm for $210,000. Commenting upon the
shrewdness of the effort which the Archdiocese's lawyers
have made to strike the case from the records as soon as

Frank and Laura (Charlotte Rampling).

possible, Frank replies, "It just struck me how neatly three
goes into this amount. That means I'd keep seventy....
So that's it--I take the money--and no one will ever know
the truth: that that girl was turned into a vegetable because of two doctors' negligence and that rather than face
what they did they'd rather buy me off to keep my mouth
shut about it." Handing back the check, Frank declares,
"If I take the money, I'm lost--I'll just be a rich ambulance
chaser." Like Paul Biegler in Anatomy, Frank recognizes
his obligation as a lawyer to see to it that justice is done at
any and all costs.

Now that he has decided to take the case to court,
Frank must secure the aid of his friend Mickey. Mickey
objects: "The reason I got you the case was because of
the money." He also warns Frank that the attorney for the
Archdiocese is none other than the "prince of darkness"
himself, Ed Concannon (James Mason). However, Frank remains determined to fight for what he sees as the truth.
Finally, Mickey reluctantly consents to help him out.
Whereas in Anatomy the strength of the hero's case depended largely upon the redemption of his alcoholic col-
league, here everything hangs upon the ability of the hero
himself, Galvin, to abandon his sodden lifestyle and pull
himself together.

The attorney for the defense, Concannon, like Claude
Dancer of Anatomy--and, to a certain extent, Hans Rolfe in
Judgment at Nuremberg, Jonathan Wilk in Compulsion, and
Matthew Harrison Brady in Inherit the Wind--is the traditional super-lawyer type: shrewd, slick, obviously the
product of a prestigious law school, and surrounded by
"yes-men"--although Concannon has at least a dozen,
whereas Dancer had only Mitch Lodwick. Lumet provides
an amusing contrast between the relative powers of the two
lawyers Galvin and Concannon by cutting from a conference
between Concannon and his dozen junior partners in his
luxurious office to a shot of Frank and Mickey sitting at a
small table in a corner of a musty old library, searching in
vain for evidence to support their case (recall Paul and
Parnell in Anatomy). However, here we are given a look
at the preparatory tactics of both sides, whereas in Anatomy we only got a glimpse of those of the defense in an attempt to get us to side with "humble country lawyer" Biegler and his sidekick. In The Verdict the contrast is not as

Sidney Lumet discusses a scene with Paul Newman.

clear-cut--both Galvin and Concannon are Boston lawyers--
but Galvin is still seen as the underdog. However, we shall
see that honesty, hard work, and determination are not the
only methods Galvin will employ in the name of justice.

We are also shown in The Verdict, much more extensively than in Anatomy, how a lawyer "coaches" his client to
perfect a style of responding to questions that will appear
dignified and authoritative to a jury and thereby secure
their sympathies. This was only hinted at in Anatomy when
Duane Miller stated that Lodwick and Dancer took some of
the prisoners from the jail into their office for a "conference" before the trial began. In The Verdict, when Dr.
Towler, the physician on trial who treated Kaye, offers a
complicated medical explanation of what happened to her,
Concannon interrupts: "Cut the bullshit, please. Just say
it--she threw up in her mask." Later, when Galvin has
Towler on the stand, the recalling of this moment provides
a break in the tension: Galvin asks Towler whether the
medical terminology describing Kaye's condition is correct,

and Towler deliberately translates Galvin's question into lay-
man's terms for the benefit of the jury by replying, "Yes,
she threw up in her mask."

It is at about this time that Galvin, still confident that
he has a strong case behind him, returns to the pinball
machine and runs up a high score, which elicits a shout of
triumph from this figure who, last time we saw him play,
had seemed as though he would remain a permanent washout.
Obviously, the pinball machine is intended to represent the
legal system, a game that some manage to beat and control
while others watch fearfully as the ball drops into the last
hole.

Galvin's enthusiasm begins to fade, however, when he
meets Judge Hoyle (Milo O'Shea), who has a reputation for
favoring defendants and who would rather see Galvin take
the money and make his plea for justice somewhere else.

Galvin begins to wish he'd done just that when he
tries to round up witnesses: Dr. Gruber, his star witness,
has suddenly left for the Caribbean (we later discover that
he was bought off by Concannon) and Maureen Rooney
(Julie Bovasso), a scrub nurse who was present during
Deborah Kaye's childbirth, would sooner forget the whole
ordeal and scorns Galvin's intentions: "You lawyers are all
the same. You don't care who you hurt so long as you can
make a buck--you're a bunch of whores."

Frank's only hope is a Dr. Thompson, a 74-year-old
M.D. at a woman's hospital in New York who specializes in
anesthesiology. The fact that he is black worries Galvin,
who fears that some of the jury members may be prejudiced
(recall Parnell's disappointment at the youthful, naive appearance of Dr. Smith in Anatomy: "I thought you'd be
older [and hence more experienced-looking], with glasses
and a limp, maybe"--and also his statement to Manion that a
doctor with a "good German name" sits better with a jury).

Frank's worst fears are confirmed once the trial begins. Judge Hoyle, in an obviously biased attempt to discredit Galvin's only witness, Dr. Thompson, interrupts Galvin's questioning and forces Thompson to admit that Doctors
Towler and Marx's failure to restore Kaye's heartbeat within
a few minutes does not in itself constitute negligence on their

part. Negligence, the reader will recall, is precisely the
core of Galvin's case. Galvin, outraged at the judge's attempt to dismiss his whole case against the doctors within
such a narrow context, snaps, "Your honor, with all due
respect, if you're going to try my case for me I wish you
wouldn't lose it." Galvin's efforts to cross-examine Dr.
Towler prove futile as his failure to recall that Kaye was
anemic is used by Towler to refute Galvin's inquiry regarding the time it took for the victim to develop brain damage.
"You broke the first rule they taught you in law school,"
Mickey reminds Frank. "Never ask a question unless you
already know the answer."

It looks as though it's all over--temporarily, anyway.
Frank has lost much of his self-confidence, but nevertheless
he refuses to give up. Mickey: "There'll be other cases,
Frankie." Frank: "There are no other cases. This is the
case. This is the case." And sure enough, after much
persistence, they uncover the name of one Kaitlin Costello,
the admitting nurse at the hospital and the only one present
at the time of the incident whose testimony is not on record.
Frank shrewdly tricks Maureen Rooney, a friend of Costello,
into revealing her whereabouts: New York City. Using

Milo O'Shea, James Mason, and Paul Newman.

innumerable aliases, Frank and Mickey telephone various
nursing agencies in the Big Apple in an attempt to locate
Costello, but to no avail.

Days go by without even a clue, when the arrival of
Frank's phone bill gives him an idea. He breaks into Rooney's mailbox, locates her bill, scans it, and notes several
calls to the same number in New York City. Under the guise
of a representative from a nursing magazine, Frank dials the
number, and, sure enough, Costello (now married and going
by the name Price) answers. He discovers that she works
at a child-care center and immediately hops aboard the next
flight to New York. He persuades her to come to Boston and
testify for him.

While in New York, Frank is informed by Mickey that
Laura Fischer (Charlotte Rampling), the woman who has been
his guiding force--and love interest--throughout the case, is
in the employ of Concannon. Lumet's handling of the revelation is reminiscent of the scene in Kazan's On the Waterfront where Marlon Brando tells Eva Marie Saint that he is
responsible for her brother's death amid the sounds of boats
in the local harbor. Mickey and Frank (standing on a side-
walk facing each other) are shown in long shot from high
above, and their dialogue is completely blocked out by the
noise of the city. Galvin proceeds immediately to a local bar
and, finding Laura there, promptly socks her across the jaw.

Refusing a mistrial, Frank returns to court confident
that Nurse Costello's testimony alone will win his case for
him--indeed, it will have to, for it is all he has left. The
prosecution produces a copy of Kaye's medical chart, signed
by Costello, stating that Kaye was anesthetized nine hours
after eating. However, Costello testifies that she did not
write a "9" in the space, but rather a "1," which, as Dr.
Towler himself has admitted, would mean that the administering of an anesthetic constituted an illegal medical procedure. Costello claims that Dr. Towler had performed five
difficult deliveries that day prior to the Kaye one, and that
in his exhaustion he had forgotten to check Kaye's chart before proceeding with the labor. After the disastrous delivery,
in order to avoid a malpractice suit, he ordered Costello to
change the "1" to a "9" or he would see to it that she lost
her job. Much to Concannon's astonishment--when he tries
to nail the witness for perjury--she produces a photocopy of

Frank questions Kaitlin Costello Price (Lindsay Crouse) about
the discrepancy with the photocopies.

the original form with a "1" written on it. However, one of
Concannon's men manages to locate a precedent which states
that a photocopy is inadmissible evidence because of the possibility of tampering. The judge accepts Concannon's objection. Concannon further argues that Costello's testimony
regarding the doctor's statements goes beyond her function
as a rebuttal witness--namely, to confine herself to discussing only the chart itself--and that since the chart has been
ruled inadmissible her entire appearance in the court should
be stricken from the records. Galvin's final blow comes when
Judge Hoyle again rules in Concannon's favor.

     Frank's last chance to gain the sympathy of the jury
is through his summation. He makes a valiant effort, appeal-
ing to the jury's innate decency by reminding them that

Concannon attempts to nail Costello for perjury.

> The rich win, the poor are powerless ... we be-
> come victims because we doubt ourselves, our insti-
> tutions, the law ... <u>you</u> are the law, not the law-
> yers, not some book, not a marble statue--those
> are only symbols of our <u>desire</u> to be just, a fervent
> and frightened prayer ... if we are to have faith in
> justice we have only to believe in ourselves.

The jury miraculously rules in Galvin's favor--obviously because their belief in the sincerity of Costello's testimony
has caused them to disregard the judge's request that it be
stricken from the records (recall that in <u>Anatomy</u> Biegler
had reminded Manion that it is impossible for a jury to disregard testimony once they've heard it). As Dr. Thompson
had remarked earlier, "Sometimes people have a great capacity to hear the truth."

<u>The Verdict</u> was the subject of considerable contro-
versy among members of the legal profession at the time of

its release because of its alleged depiction of "gross legal flaws" in exploring the corruptibility of the system. Aric Press of <u>Newsweek</u> summed up the opinions of the majority of lawyers who objected to the tactics used by the attorneys in the film, and his statements are worth citing here. First, with regard to the photocopy which Costello produces, Margaret Berger, an evidence authority at Brooklyn Law School, stated, "Under modern rules of evidence, duplicates are now admissible for every purpose." Also, Press added, "Since the issue [in the film] is whether the original was tampered with, the jury should have been shown both copies and allowed to reach its own conclusion. The judge must not make that decision for them."[1]

Concerning Costello's testimony: "She says the doctor told her to change the chart. That directly contradicts his defense that he correctly administered the general anesthetic since his patient had not eaten for nine hours. Therefore, says Vanderbilt law Prof. Michael Goldsmith, her statement would be well within the scope of a rebuttal witness."

With respect to the jury's verdict: "The case should never have gone to the jury. When the evidence of the surprise witness was barred, Newman's case collapsed completely: he literally had no evidence. In these circumstances, Mason would have requested a directed verdict from the judge and the judge would have been obliged to grant it."

Regarding other aspects in general: "No fancy law firm would put two-dozen lawyers on a negligence case; that full-court treatment is reserved for antitrust and merger fights. And it is hard to imagine a law firm assigning a female lawyer to seduce the opposing counsel. That's clearly unethical. In an effort to prove himself, Newman chose to go on with the trial. Most lawyers would have called for a mistrial; at the very least, that would have disqualified Mason from the case.... Mason is not the only unethical lawyer in court. Newman rejects a generous offer of settlement without consulting his client, tampers with the U.S. Mail and sits around doing nothing but drinking until just 10 days before the trial." Perhaps most damaging to the credibility of the film's outcome is Press' point that in real life Newman's case would never even have gone to the jury; the judge would have decided the matter after Costello's testimony was ruled inadmissible--and, judging from Hoyle's

attitude toward Galvin throughout the trial, it would not be
difficult to guess which side he would have favored.

These discrepancies between truth and fiction were the
result of screenwriter David Mamet's overzealous desire to
provide an accurate expose on the corruptibility of the system. But his efforts have served more often than not to
defeat his own purpose. If his main concern is the redemption of Galvin, having him resort to illegal methods of obtaining evidence is hardly an effective means of securing
audience sympathy for him.

But then, the unattractiveness of the Galvin character arises as a result of the combined efforts of Mamet, who
created Galvin based on Barry Reed's original conception,
and of Paul Newman, who plays him. The Frank Galvin
presented by Mamet and Newman is essentially a pathetic,
washed-up, bitter alcoholic--nothing more. We are not given
any indication that the man possesses an innate sense of
decency--such as evidenced by James Stewart as Biegler--
which his drunkenness is suppressing. Consequently, we
are reluctant to agree that he deserves one last chance to
redeem himself. Newman's Galvin (an example of casting-
against-type) walks about the majority of the time with a
look of giddy bemusement at the seriousness of the situation
to which he has become irrevocably attached. However, he
does a believable job of looking physically and emotionally at
wit's end when it seems as though everything has turned
against him (one is almost tempted to compare his attitude at
this point with James Stewart's suicidal frustration in Capra's
It's a Wonderful Life [1946]).

The outlook of the film in general seems intended to
reflect the pessimism of 1980s America, where there are no
real winners or losers--just self-centered, highly biased individuals who have grown disenchanted with society and who
could care less about helping their fellow man. This is best
exemplified in the scene where Galvin, in desperation after
discovering that all his witnesses have deserted him the day
before the trial is scheduled to begin, rushes to Judge
Hoyle's home late at night to ask for a postponement of the
proceedings. Hoyle adamantly refuses to hear him out, eye-
ing him contemptuously and sneering, "I have no sympathy
for you." Years of bickering with lawyers for the prosecution have tainted Hoyle's outlook on them.

We soon discover that several of the other characters have also adopted selfish perspectives on life based on past experiences. Concannon's main concern, as he tells Laura, is to "win at all costs--nothing else matters." To Laura and Mickey, money is of the utmost importance on their list of values. The Bishop of the Archdiocese, as mentioned before, is concerned only with protecting his reputation.

Under the topic of societal pessimism come the numerous references to common attitudes about professions which abound in David Mamet's screenplay. The Doneghys, referring to Kaye's condition, tell Galvin that "Nobody cares"--when in fact they themselves are seeking to evade responsibility for her care; Galvin remarks of the jury that they've all come into court pumped with the notion that you can't fight City Hall; when Mr. Doneghy discovers that Galvin has turned down the settlement that would enable him and his wife to escape to the West Coast, his sentiments echo those of Maureen Rooney: "You're all the same. You tell us you'll do the best you can, and then when you screw up it's, 'Oh, I'm dreadfully sorry. I did the best I could.' And people like us live with your mistakes the rest of our lives."

Helping most to convey the gloomy atmosphere of the film are the cinematography of Andrzej Bartkowiak, the production design of Edward Prisoni, and the direction of Sidney Lumet. Using real-life locations (including Manhattan's Tweed Courthouse and the Massachusetts State House in Boston), they have fashioned a Boston which is, as John Simon remarked, "a truly obsolescent city, situated in a no-man's-land between past and present ... [the] settings manage to be actively but understatedly unsettling ... an indeterminate gloom pervades not only the grizzled interiors but even the exteriors, where faces emerge from a dismal, almost grimy, darkness, which reluctantly yields them up to a sparse beam of light that barely fits them--like old clothes grown too tight."[2]

As of late (since Lumet began his collaboration with Bartkowiak) the atmosphere in Lumet's features has become increasingly heavy and somber, with very little music. This fortunately did not harm The Verdict, but his next feature, Daniel (1983) suffered considerably from slow pacing and plodding exposition. Under Lumet's guidance, The Verdict

moves along at a steady but decidedly leisurely rate, allowing time for a thorough examination of all the principal characters (as in Anatomy) before the trial begins (shots of Newman leaning over the pinball machine in the bar in silence
seem to linger in the mind). While this helps the viewer to
come to grips with the plight of the characters in the story,
after some two hours and ten minutes, in light of the dismal
outlook on society which the film presents, one is left with
a rather unpleasant taste in his mouth (most of the film feels
like the funeral parlor depicted at the outset). Fortunately,
as John Simon points out, "Afterward, it all evaporates from
the memory with merciful celerity."

Lumet does manage to succeed very well, however, in
creating a feeling of vicarious anxiety in the viewer when
Galvin begins to grow more and more desperate as the trial
wages on. And there are also a number of dandy performances, coaxed to near-perfection by the director, to keep
the viewer from becoming completely offended by the outlook
of the film. Although Paul Newman as Galvin is only spo-
radically effective--as noted earlier--impressive performances
are given by Jack Warden as Frank's abrasive but good-
hearted buddy; James Mason as the crafty lawyer for the
defense; Milo O'Shea as the judge who is dead-set against
Frank Galvin from the start; Charlotte Rampling as Frank's
unfeeling love interest; and Edward Binns, Julie Bovasso,
and Lindsay Crouse as the Bishop, Maureen Rooney, and
Kaitlin Costello, respectively. Indeed, it comes as no great
surprise that the ensemble acting in uniformly first-rate
when one considers that nearly all of the principals (including Mason, Rampling, Binns, and Warden) had worked with
Lumet on at least one occasion over the previous two decades; this was no haphazardly chosen collection of actors.

As of this writing (spring 1986) The Verdict remains
the last courtroom drama from Hollywood to successfully up-
date the traditional themes and motifs of its predecessors to
modern terms. Once again, in the character of Galvin, we
have the dedicated (anti-) hero (reminiscent of Henry Fonda
in 12 Angry Men, Charles Laughton in Witness for the
Prosecution, Orson Welles in Compulsion, James Stewart
in Anatomy of a Murder, and Spencer Tracy in Inherit
the Wind and Judgment at Nuremberg) determined to fight
for Justice at any cost. Again, there is the preoccupation
with the fairness of the jury system (12 Angry Men, Anatomy)

and the crusading attempt to expose dangerous evils in society (12 Angry Men, I Want to Live!, Compulsion). Peter
Hyams' 1983 Star Chamber, which chronicled the attempts
of one judge to rebel against a too-lenient system by form-
ing a secret judicial society, was an admirable try at the
crusading format of courtroom drama, but ultimately it proved
too unbelievable and predictable to really deserve serious
consideration here. This is not to say, however, that The
Verdict is without its faults--it admittedly lacks the charm
of Witness for the Prosecution and the accuracy of judgment
of Anatomy of a Murder, among other things. However,
its box-office success confirms the fact that today's audiences
still share a desire to see the age-old conflicts of good versus
evil, Justice versus injustice, and power versus truth acted
out before their eyes via the grandest form of entertainment
known to man--the silver screen.

NOTES

1. Aric Press, "The Verdict: A Legal Opinion," Newsweek,
    February 28, 1983, p. 51.

2. John Simon, review of The Verdict in National Review,
    February 4, 1983, p. 132.

NAME INDEX

FILM TITLE INDEX